Tasks

Creating a Rite of Passage

by

Jack Taylor and Shel Arensen

www.12tasks.org

Dedicated to all who have dared to complete the 12 Tasks
and those who will soon make the effort.

PREFACE

I (Jack) think most of us stumble into adulthood. When I was twelve, I didn't think of adulthood. Life moved from one thing to the next. From grade school to high school. From one sports team to the next. From one rank in boys club to the next. Life was safe, stable, hopeful and I was naïve and eager to engage in the adventures offered by my parents. Or so they thought.

But life has changed. Hasn't it?

Children still grow into adults. They come of age like they have in every generation. They navigate the turbulent seas of adolescence with trustworthy guides and mentors and they have clear milestones to let them know when they have succeeded – right?

I'm not so sure. When I was growing up, what I did often determined how I identified myself. Like every child, I was asked what did I want to be when I grew up? I wanted to be a doctor, a lawyer, an astronaut, a politician, an athlete, a mechanic, a pastor, a teacher, a parent, etc. and when I'd finished my studies that was who I was. Now, children are faced with considering who they are first (meaning gender, race, orientation) and what they do may fluctuate from season to season in their life.

What worth would you place on knowing that you could build lasting confidence into the soul of your son or daughter? That you could set their feet on a guided path toward greater resiliency, increasing wisdom, fewer regrets and perhaps a life of hope-filled faith? And what if you could build a stronger enduring relationship with your child to keep them anchored during the years of their troubled teens? What if you could raise and influence the next generation of world changers in a culture that is increasingly volatile, uncertain, complex and ambiguous?

Shel and I are both authors of numerous books, which use a narrative arc to show the transformation of the protagonist's character. This 'hero' of the story launches out from their everyday life when some problem shakes them awake and beckons them forward. During the adventure they meet a trustworthy guide to carry them through what is ahead. A plan is embraced and through various successes and failures the quest is achieved.

We believe that children in our world continue to be thrust into the adventure of growing up that youngsters have been facing for generations. However, we believe they have lost some of the essential markers toward adulthood along the way. There are quandaries, problems and challenges in our contemporary world that our parents and grandparents never faced.

Adulthood is being delayed as more and more youngsters stumble around the journey of life facing enigmas, dilemmas, detours and quicksand quandaries, looking for an elusive treasure. Whether distracted parents, overpowering media, alluring peers, economic uncertainty, social fears or contemporary world views have created all this – the reality still exists. There seems to be no clear path forward to adulthood.

Children don't seem to know how to navigate the essential milestones toward adulthood and parents don't seem to know how to guide them. We believe there is a God-given chance to change this.

Mothers may be more sensitive to the struggles, choices and desires of their children but fathers are also essential in any intentional mentoring toward adulthood. Shel and I found that mentoring our sons and daughters helped to ground them, orient them in a positive direction and solidify their confidence for the turbulent teen years ahead.

This is our story, our sons' and daughters' stories, and their sons' and daughters' stories. We share it with you as an invitation to make a difference as your son or daughter launches out on one of the most important adventures of their life – becoming an adult. We share life tips through story, exercises and wisdom learned from experience. We hope your adventure as parent and child becomes as meaningful and life-impacting as it was for us.

INTRODUCTION

Walking Your Son or Daughter into Adulthood

This book was birthed out of a journey we (the authors) each took with our own sons and daughters. The experience proved to have such a lasting impact that our adult children are now passing it on to their children – our grandchildren! Other parents around the world have heard about 12 Tasks and its value. Many have adapted it for themselves, while others have asked how to do 12 Tasks or requested a resource for leading their children on the path to adulthood. We finally decided it was time to write a book for them and any other parents who need support in helping their children transition to adulthood.

We wrote this book because we are fathers who are passionate about helping our children and grandchildren make a successful transition from being youth to being adults. And we sense there are many parents who feel the same passion but need something personal and practical to help them on the journey.

Boys and girls are growing up who seem to be without clear direction, firm commitments, moral integrity, spiritual discernment, financial awareness and a sense of their own individual responsibility to the world in which they live. As Atlanta pastor Andy Stanley notes – parents are caught in the tension between the real and the ideal while they prepare children for their future.

A son or daughter must understand who they are, why they are, what they are here for and where they are going. For that to happen the parent must work out the answers to these issues in advance for themselves. Part of the chaos and confusion of our society stems from the lack of carefully thought-out answers by the generations already establishing educational, political, spiritual and social templates for those who come behind them.

Can this generation of parents do anything to help this generation of youth into adulthood in a rapidly changing world?

We offer 12 Tasks as a simple tool that you and your emerging adult can use for your journey. 12 Tasks is not an easy journey. It will require a lot from both of you and a dedication to see it through when times get tough. There is no real formula for success when it comes to growing up, but an intentional parent (or adult-figure) makes a big difference. We truly believe 12 Tasks can help deepen your relationship between parent and child and strengthen your son or daughter's transition toward adulthood.

This book includes the journey that Richard and I [Jack] took together in what we dubbed the 12 Tasks of Manhood. The experience proved to have such a lasting impact on Richard that he asked that we share this with other fathers looking to help their sons. Since we [my wife Gayle and I] replicated the feat with our daughters in the 12 Tasks of Womanhood you will see examples from that journey with Michelle and Laura.

This book also traces the history of 12 Tasks, going back to 1991 when my (Shel's) wife Kym came up with the idea to guide our first son Heath up the slippery path to adulthood. Since then Kym and I helped our other two sons and our daughter to complete 12 Tasks. And in the past few years, we've enjoyed watching our adult children leading our grandchildren through their own unique set of 12 Tasks.

We have since discovered there are many other parents who felt this void of guided transition. Some have asked us how to do 12 Tasks. Others have created their own options. We offer 12 Tasks as one pathway to consider for those who are willing to invest significant time and energy to build a lasting bond and a solid Christian character in both parent and young teen.

Wise parents steward the maturing of their young ones with an emphasis on relationship more than on rules and experiences.

12 Tasks is not just a one-day event for the son or daughter, although there is a significant one-day experience to celebrate the completion of these tasks. It is a one-year journey taken together at a crucial time of a young person's life. It is a journey that involves significant others who provide affirmation and confirmation and mentoring along the way.

I [Jack] feel that this experience built a lasting bond that continues to this day. Memories of the past are more than pasted pictures in an album of celebration. They are foundation stones that still speak into my life when I face new challenges for myself or with those I lead. I hear this reality still echoing in the life of my son and daughters.

For those of you who engage through story, we have portrayed the journey in the lives of other fathers and sons. For those of you who just want the how-to manual in brief, we have it here. We need world changers who will outlive any of our expectations and all they need is ability, opportunity and motivation.

We invite you on a journey you won't regret.

Jack Taylor (PhD), British Columbia
Shel Arensen, Naivasha, Kenya
August 2021

PART

BACKGROUND

Where 12 Tasks Began

(Shel) have to give credit to my wife, Kym 'I have an idea' Arensen, for starting 12 Tasks. In January 1991 we lived at Kijabe, Kenya, a mission station on the edge of the Rift Valley. Our oldest son, Heath, would have his 12th birthday in February. We had noticed his lack of confidence – in school and other activities. As a young boy, he'd had one grand mal seizure and for a number of years doctors had him on anti-seizure medication. This led to him thinking he was not smart and couldn't succeed at school. Thankfully, after much prayer and then some treatment from a Christian chiropractor, we'd been able to take Heath off his medication. But he still had lingering doubts on his ability. As we pondered how to encourage Heath to live to his full potential, Kym came up with the idea of 12 Tasks.

I had studied the various rites of passage practiced by the Agikuyu people who lived around us at Kijabe, as well as similar ceremonies practiced by the Maasai who lived in the valley in front of us. As an editor for *Today in Africa*, a Christian youth magazine, I had noted how Christian youth in Kenya had lost touch with some of their traditions that had provided valuable meaning in their culture. Perhaps the most crucial ceremony was the coming of age rite of passage, which involved circumcision for boys around the age of 12 or 13 and a similar ceremony for girls. It was the way these young people marked the end of childhood and the beginning of the next stage of their life. Mwaura Njoroge, my editor-in-training, and I had written a novel on this issue called *Against the Traditions*.

As Kym and I had discussed what I'd learned and how Christian African families could create alternate rites of passage, Kym wondered if we could create a rite of passage for Heath? What if we gave him a list of challenges he had to accomplish before he turned 13? As he learned to complete these challenges, perhaps he would build the confidence he needed to succeed as he moved towards manhood.

Over a cup of tea on our veranda overlooking the iconic crater of Mt Longonot, Kym and I sat down and brainstormed what these challenges would look like. It was his 12th birthday. What if we chose 12 tasks? It had a certain ring to it, harking back to the 12 tasks of Hercules from Greek mythology. In our bookshelf we also had a copy of the cartoon book *The 12 Tasks of Asterix*, based on the 1976 film from the comic book series that we all enjoyed reading.[1]

There were 12 months in a year, so it would be possible to complete one task a month before Heath's 13th birthday. But what kind of tasks would we choose? We believed faith in God was the central platform on which to build a life, so we wanted some tasks that would motivate Heath to grow spiritually. Kym wrote down the ideas as they bubbled out. An inductive Bible study to show Heath how to read and study the Bible for himself. Heath had a hard time memorizing. So a task of memorizing certain Bible passages would stretch him and show him he could memorize – and he would have Scripture in his heart to chew on.

How about some tasks to challenge Heath's mental skills? We chose a reading list of books.

We lived in Africa, but Kijabe sometimes seemed like an isolated bubble – a little bit of North America and Europe dropped into the middle of Africa. We wanted Heath to appreciate the culture of Africa. What about a task that involved living with a Kenyan family for a few nights so he could have a first-hand experience of a traditional Kenyan family?

---

1   Rene Goscinny, The Twelve Tasks of Asterix, Int'l Learning Systems, 1975, 1995.

We wanted to encourage Heath with some physical challenges to help him develop endurance and skills for playing sports and living a healthy lifestyle. Running 30 miles in 30 days was added to the list. What about climbing Mt Kenya? That would take planning and strength and endurance. Maybe it could be the final task. We wrote it down.

Life skills? We enjoyed camping as a family. But could Heath survive a night camping in the forest below our house by himself? Could he set up his own tent, plan and buy his own food and then start a fire to cook his own meal? The solo camp-out went onto our list.

We wanted to teach and encourage Heath about the importance of sexual purity as part of his 12 Tasks. We hit on the idea of a special meal after he had completed the other 11 tasks, where I could share with him God's plan for a man and a wife. One of the 12 Tasks of Asterix and his rotund friend Obelix that tickled our boys from the cartoon book was the sixth task – to finish a meal by Mannekinpix, the famous Belgian chef who cooked gigantic meals for the Titans. Obelix breezes through this task, polishing off a boar and fries, a flock of geese, several sheep, an omelette made from eight dozen eggs, a school of fish, an ox, a cow, a huge mound of caviar on a single piece of toast, a camel and, finally, an elephant stuffed with olives.

We didn't have a Belgian chef called Mannekinpix, but Nairobi had a well-known restaurant called The Carnivore. It boasted all-the-meat-you-can-eat, grilled on long Maasai swords over a gigantic grill. When you sat at the table, they gave you a small paper flag. As long as the flag stood up, the waiters would come by your table and slice off slabs of meat. In addition to beef, pork and chicken, they also served a variety of wild game meat – zebra, ostrich, eland, impala, kongoni – even crocodile. When you could eat no more, you had to surrender and lower your flag.

We decided the final task would be to finish a meat feast at the Carnivore, followed by a father-to-son talk on sexual purity.

After we had winnowed our ideas down to 12 challenging but doable tasks, Kym created a blank photo album book with each task listed at the top of the page. Each page left space for photos or mementos of that particular task. Kym and I each wrote a letter to Heath, explaining why he was receiving this challenging birthday present and pasted our letters near the beginning of the 12 Tasks Book.

Part of Kym's letter went like this: "Dear Heath, God has given your Dad and I a great privilege in helping to guide you towards adulthood. God's desire for you is to become fully mature – spiritually, physically, emotionally, mentally...Your Dad and I have asked God's wisdom in preparing these tasks for you to help you press on towards maturity. Remember, God is with you – depend on him and his strength. Don't try to do this on your own..."

Here's my letter: *"Dear Heath, You are 12 years old today. As you approach your teen years and becoming a man, you will face many new and challenging situations... To give you the confidence to know that you can accomplish things, we have given you some jobs, some tasks to do this year. To complete them will require all your skills and strength. They will require you to turn to God for help. They will stretch you. You will do things you didn't think possible. And at the end of the year, with the Lord's help, you will have the confidence to face the years ahead, knowing that you have conquered the tasks of manhood."*

At Heath's 12th birthday we had his friends over and after the games, birthday cake and presents, we told Heath we had one last special gift. After he opened up his 12 Tasks book, we explained how we would work with him to help him complete everything before his 13th birthday, when he would become a man.

I remember Heath looking rather dismayed at first, as he digested the things he would be expected to do in the coming year. He shirked at the idea of having to run 30 miles in 30 days. He didn't feel he could memorize the required verses. I'm not sure what he felt about the requirement of learning some basic rock climbing skills and scaling Fischer's Tower in Hell's Gate National Park. But he really wanted to climb Mt Kenya and couldn't wait for the task, where we'd written: Thou art challenged to eat an Obelix meal at the Carnivore.

That next year wasn't easy for Heath, or for us. We started with the running task, but he balked at running every day. I had to run alongside him and keep pushing him on. He became angry with me. But he did persevere and completed his tasks, including the three-day hike to Pt Lenana at 16,000 feet on Mt Kenya.

For his 13th birthday, we invited his friends, his teachers and other significant adults in his life. We shared with everyone how Heath had completed his 12 tasks and Heath showed everyone his book, which memorialized the year. We declared that he had become a man and gave him a red Swiss army knife with multiple blades and tools, a symbolic gift that he was old enough and responsible enough to keep and use this knife.

Going through the 12 Tasks of manhood as a rite of passage did not magically make Heath's transition to adulthood easy. There were still struggles. But often, as we talked and worked through various issues, we could look back at the things he had learned during his 12th year, and that gave Heath courage and strength to carry on.

We have four children. So once Heath had completed his tasks, his brother Reid wanted to know what his tasks would be, as did our next son, Blake, and finally our daughter Malindi. The task list varied for each child, but climbing Mt Kenya, the solo campout and the special meal and purity talk made the list for each of our kids.

To our amazement, within a year or two other missionary couples from Kijabe, including our friends Jack and Gayle Taylor, had taken our idea and adapted and improved it for their own children. I later wrote one of my children's adventure novels around the 12 Tasks, calling the book *The Test of the*

Tribal Challenge. It was a fictional story, combining the accounts from the lives of our kids. As a result, the idea of 12 Tasks of adulthood has moved around the world, with spinoffs and personal touches added by creative caring parents.

One of the most touching came when my friend Mwaura Njoroge told me that he was doing 12 Tasks with his son Mutoria. They had already climbed Mt Kenya. Mwaura asked if Mutoria could live with us for a few days as his cultural task. It was payback time, as Heath and Blake had spent some nights at Mwaura's parents' farm in Solai as part of their 12 Tasks, learning to eat Kenyan food, spraying tomatoes in the field and getting voluminous hugs from Mwaura's mother. Heath had even acted as the conductor on a matatu, calling out for passengers and collecting the fares for an overloaded Kenyan rural taxi. So we invited Mutoria into our home for a few days, even taking him on a boat ride on Lake Naivasha. When his father picked him up a few days later, Mutoria ran and hugged his Dad. He had survived his hardest task – living with a white American family! He told his Dad he'd thought he might die on the boat and Mr. Arensen had spread way too much plum jam on his toast every morning!

So that's where 12 Tasks started. It began with a concern to see our children mature and grow in faith, in mind and in stature. And it borrowed from the rites of passage we saw in the cultures around us in Africa. We believe 12 Tasks can be a valuable tool in preparing your child for becoming an adult in a rapidly changing world.

***

As Shel mentioned, my wife Gayle and I (Jack) heard what the Arensens had done with their sons Heath and Reid. It's likely Gayle's friendship with Kym got the ball rolling for us. Richard was a classmate of Reid's at the Rift Valley Academy so we had a similar concern to engage in the process of motivating our son toward manhood. I was taking some courses in African

Traditional Religion from Shel's brother Jon and understood the importance of local rites of passage. As a seminary grad, I was also familiar with the Bar Mitzvah practices of the Jews. The 12 Tasks of Asterix had been on our reading list as well.

Like Heath, Richard had some confidence issues. We wanted our son to own the 12 Tasks he would have to accomplish, so we deliberately enlarged our list to 16 and had him choose the 12 he wanted to accomplish. We divided the tasks into the categories of Spiritual, Mental, Physical and Social with a focus on improving strengths, stimulating growth, broadening relationships and experiencing new things. Of course, later we developed tasks for Michelle and Laura.

One aspect that was important to me was the opportunity to build a stronger bond with my son or daughter by doing some of the tasks together in areas where neither of us was comfortable nor competent. There is something vulnerable and authentic about entering into a challenge where you aren't naturally the gifted or experienced leader. There is some mutual dependency but also a testing of character where limits expose you at a deeper level. Climbing Mt Kenya and building a tree fort were two of these tasks. Climbing the mountain with other sons, daughters and dads added to the memorable energy and adventure.

Ancient cultures have significant trials to mark the passage into adulthood. What would it be like in our world if we broadened our concepts and definitions of maturity to include bravery, responsibility, self-control, gentleness, discipline, patience, generosity, empathy toward others, self-sacrifice, trustworthiness etc. and what if we set up specific opportunities that would challenge and test our children toward adulthood?

We, too, adopted the idea of a final celebration where we invited close friends and adults to see the results of the year. This was followed by a retreat away and a talk on purity followed by the giving of a purity ring. I took my son and my wife took my daughters when their time arrived. It was a time of growth for all of us.

Since our return to North America, we have encountered

other movements designed to encourage this rite of passage. We offer the 12 Tasks as one option that worked for our children

Jack sees another side to why 12 Tasks are important for both boys and girls.

Of all the creative mysteries of God, from the transformation of darkness into light, of caterpillar into Monarch, of first glance to life-long love, there is none so magical for a parent as watching their child transform into an adult. From car seat to driver's seat the adventure is one that will test every element of wisdom and hope we might have for the next generation. At least that's our dream until life changes the script.

To observe and participate in the process of a youth moving from seeing only through their own eyes to seeing through the eyes of another; from selfishly taking to sacrificially giving; from blankness to understanding; from weakness to strength; from frustration to triumph; from fear to hope... there is nothing so mysterious for a parent to experience with their child.

It's the unseen things that make the difference. A sculptor can recreate the perfect features of a person, but they can't breathe life into that work of art. They can choose clay or marble or ice as a medium, but they can't turn what looks like an adult into a real adult. That takes more than what you can manipulate with your hand.

Most societies have framed markers and ceremonies for this path of transformation. In western culture, our preoccupation with individualism appears to have hijacked a feature which can serve to breathe life into the next generation of heroes. Great currents of social change have eroded the traditional banks that marked the shores of former years.

Absent parents and dysfunctional families are becoming the norm in many communities. Even in homes where parents are committed, the understanding of a parent's role in the transformation of their child into adulthood can be lacking.

The past is ignored, the future is avoided, and the present is wasted.

"Research indicates that regardless of socioeconomic backgrounds, race, or location, parents of teens experience a relatively consistent set of emotions that leave many perplexed and exhausted."[2]

Can this generation of parents do anything for this generation of youth to help them into adulthood? Especially in a world that is changing so quickly.

Apologists have often pointed out that we humans must have answers to questions of origin, purpose, meaning and destiny. A parent has a unique opportunity to assist in the shaping of the answers craved by the one created in their own image. A son or daughter must understand who they are, why they are, what they are here for and where they are going. For that to happen the parent must work out the answers to these issues in advance for themselves. Part of the chaos and confusion of our society stems from the lack of carefully thought-out answers by the generations already establishing educational, political, spiritual and social templates for those who come behind them.

One of the factors we don't want to ignore early is that when God created humans as male and female the difference was more than just anatomical. In James Dobson's work *Bringing up Boys* he offers this insight, which parents might keep in mind.[3] While his comments may sound somewhat sexist in today's culture, it is still good to recognize his intent in drawing attention to the inborn differences between boys and girls when establishing tasks. I consider these statements in understanding why both parents have a role to play in the 12 Tasks.

Dobson states: "Consider again the basic tendencies of maleness and femaleness. Because it is the privilege and blessing of women to bear children, they are inclined toward

2   Jeramy and Jerusha Clark, Your Teenager is Not Crazy, (Baker: Grand Rapids, IL, 2016), p.11
3   James Dobson, Bringing Up Boys: Practical advice and encouragement for those shaping the next generation of men (Tyndale: Wheaton, ILL, 2001), p. 27

A Father Buys into 12 Tasks

For the 12 Tasks to continue there has to be buy in and sometimes that takes time and memory. Here is what Richard Taylor wrote about how, some six years ago, he realized he needed to do 12 Tasks with his sons.

I thought I was supposed to be a father of girls, sweet little girls who sat still on their daddy's lap, wore pink bows in their hair, and needed me to intimidate interested suitors, and eventually, on a day far in the future, to walk them down the aisle.

Well, God didn't give me sugar and spice and all that's nice. He gave me slugs and snails and puppy-dog's tails. He gave me gravity-defying, house-shaking, daddy-wrestling little boys.

It is a beautiful spring evening. My son Jordan is swinging as high as he can and yelling at the top of his lungs, just for the fun of it. My son Anderson is throwing a pail full of rocks down the slide and screeching with delight. My son Micah is sneaking up military style on our back yard chickens.

We sit down for a BBQ supper. Micah is strapped firmly in his chair and demanding his food by pounding on his tray. The other two never stop moving. Jordan sings while bouncing between half sitting, standing, and foot hopping. Anderson slides down until he nearly disappears under the table, then backs up again, takes a bite, then slides, and then to his knees, takes another bite, and stands up. As soon as they are excused, they are off like a rocket. Their energy never stops until it shifts gears temporarily into their dreams.

God helped me realize I am not a father to these boys by default. It is part of a sacred calling God has given me and my wife Ericka to love them and raise them as honorable men. And as I seek wisdom about how to raise them as God intended, the first and most obvious place for me to look was my own childhood. And the most compelling parts of that childhood, and my own transition to adulthood, was The 12 Tasks of Manhood.

[note: Richard and Ericka adopted a young girl from Rwanda in 2020 during Covid and she definitely does have pink bows in her hair.]

predictability, stability, security, caution and steadiness. Most of them value friendships and family above accomplishments or opportunities. That is why they often dislike change and resist moving from one city to another. The female temperament lends itself to nurturance, caring, sensitivity, tenderness and compassion. Those are the precise characteristics needed by their children during their developmental years. Without the softness of femininity, the world would be a more cold, legalistic and militaristic place.

"Men, on the other hand, have been designed for a different role. They value change, opportunity, risk, speculation and adventure. They are designed to provide for their families physically and to protect them from harm and danger. The apostle Paul said, 'If anyone does not provide for his relatives, and especially for his immediate family, he has denied the faith and is worse than an unbeliever' (I Timothy 5:8). This is a divine assignment. Men are also ordained in Scripture for leadership in their homes, to be expressed within the frame of servanthood. Men are often (but not always) less emotional in a crisis and more confident when challenged. A world without men would be more static and uninteresting."

Jeramy and Jerusha Clark add this helpful parameter to consider:

The explosive growth of neurons during childhood slow as puberty approaches. Ultimately – somewhere between the ages of eleven (for girls) and twelve and a half (for boys) – the brain shifts course and begins to prune neurons, cutting back unused brain pathways. Those neural pathways that remain are strengthened in a process called myelination continue throughout adolescence and result in what scientists describe as a wholesale, progressive remodeling of the brain.[4]

---

4   Clark, Ibid, p. 17.

Boys and girls both need guidance to become who they were designed to be without pre-confining them into specific roles, tasks, interests, strengths or weaknesses. 12 Tasks gives you the freedom to do this.

12 Tasks - A Rite of Passage

The 12 Tasks could be described as a rite of passage. Many communities around the world had specific rites of passage, as members moved through various stages of life. Often these rites of passage were accompanied by ceremonies, rituals and traditions. One of the most important in many cultures seems to have been the coming of age ceremony.

Learning to Be Adult

Only one man and one woman were created fully mature as persons. Every other male and female on this planet, including Jesus, had to learn to become adults. Since the dawn of time, fathers and mothers have been looking back at their sons and daughters trying to discern if there are ways to make the process of becoming adults easier on the next generation.

One issue that is sometimes overlooked is the role of the community of coaches, mentors and teachers who can come alongside the father or mother to build into a son or daughter's life. Whether the issue is spiritual, emotional, intellectual, mechanical, physical or some other area of skill, there are gifted men and women who can be called on to shore up an area of life that father or mother and son or daughter want to achieve through their tasks.

Parents and youth should not have to feel like they are alone in this challenge. The network of mentors, coaches and teachers that is established will become part of the final celebration and perhaps part of a life-long support system.

A father or mother who is focused on the growth and development of their son or daughter must first do an honest analysis of who they are as adults. They must know their own strengths and abilities and they must draw out the personality and strengths of a son or daughter whom God has designed for special tasks in this world.

They must also understand what they are trying to accomplish through the 12 Tasks of Adulthood.

The 12 Tasks are meant to be a tool to create a bonding mentorship between father and son or between mother and daughter or between a child and a parent. Through the use of the 12 Tasks a parent is called on to really see the child that God has designed - to see the underlying emotional, intellectual, spiritual, physical, psychological and social realities that are preparing to emerge from the chrysalis of childhood into adulthood.

The parent is challenged to see his child's strengths and to affirm those strengths with appropriate tasks that bring confidence and awareness of his child's place in his community.

The parent is challenged to see his child's vulnerabilities and to shore those up with tasks that will build skills and hope.

The parent is challenged to see the world in which their child will grow and to design tasks which will prepare him or her for the changes still ahead.

The flexibility of the 12 Tasks allows a parent to design a wide-ranging list of tasks and to talk through this list with their son or daughter. A list of 20 different tasks could be designed and together the parent and emerging young adult may decide which ones will be pursued. The key is the balance of tasks.

The beauty of the 12 Tasks is not only in what is accomplished over a one-year period as the young person strives to embrace the challenges that have been set. The beauty is in the bonding and relationship building that is part of the process of walking your son or daughter into adulthood. During this year, other mentors may be drawn into the process so that a strong community of positive adult role models are linked to the ongoing success and well-being of this young person who is becoming a young adult.

After the formal launch of the 12 Tasks [often on the 12th or 13th birthday], a record of the year is closely monitored in pictures, records and documents. This album of growth will be a feature in the celebration event at the end of the year. This celebration event will include all close friends, other mentors and significant relations and any personalities who could be included to add impact and recognition to this occasion.

Before the final celebration event, the parent(s) and son or daughter will take a deliberate time away to discuss the purpose and practice of purity. The length and content of this time will be determined in a discussion between the parent and the young person. A purity ring will be given to the son or daughter once there is understanding and commitment to the practice of purity. This is an essential aspect of the 12 Tasks.

There are several steps in a coming of age ceremony and 12 Tasks addresses these. First, we acknowledge that the child is reaching a formative age where they will soon cross over into another era of life. When we called friends and family to each of our children's 12th birthday party, we made it clear to each child that they had reached this crossroad. And we explained to the invited guests that our child was stepping out of childhood and crossing over the threshold into adulthood. We also created a written reminder with the letter we wrote to each of our children.

The second step was to present specific challenges or tasks that our children would have to take on to prove they were ready to move on to adulthood. For our family, the 12 Tasks were presented clearly in a photo album book.

The third step was to assist our child to complete these tasks. For me (Shel), that meant four climbs up Mt Kenya, as well as some rounds of golf with my sons.

The fourth step was to celebrate the completion of the 12 Tasks. This was done in two ways. One was the 13th birthday party where we, as parents, publicly presented to friends and family what our child had completed. We showed the book with photos of the tasks. We took photos. We gave each child a special gift to commemorate their achievement. We told everyone our child had now become an adult. We conferred new responsibilities and expectations. One other way we celebrated the completion was with a special father-son or mother-daughter time. In my case, with my three sons, we celebrated with a meal at the Carnivore Restaurant in Nairobi. An integral part of the evening was a man-to-man talk about sexual purity. With my wife Kym and our daughter Malindi, they had their special time and talk on the shores of Lake Naivasha at the old Lake Hotel.

A Biblical Background for Rites of Passage

Creating a rite of passage or what is sometimes called an ARP, an alternative rite of passage, is not a concept found specifically in the Bible, but we believe it is backed up by biblical principles. When Jesus went to the temple as recorded in Luke 4:41-52, it says Jesus was 12 years old. Perhaps this was the first year he accompanied his parents to the annual Passover Festival in Jerusalem because he was coming of age. At the very least, it seems it was the first year they had given him freedom to move around without them watching his every move. In fact, they gave him so much freedom that they headed for home for a day or two before realizing he wasn't with them! It seems that in Jewish culture of that era, the age of 12 was a year when children were given more responsibility. Jesus' parents hurried back to Jerusalem, annoyed that their son had used his newfound responsibility to disappear. They found him sitting and discussing God's Word with the teachers of the law. In verse 49 Jesus said, "I had to be in my Father's house." As 12-year-old Jesus was growing in stature and wisdom and in favor with God and man, he stayed in the Temple – his Father's house.

In Proverbs 22:6 parents are urged to "Train a child in the way he should go and when he is old he will not turn from it."

Psalm 127:3-5 gives another insight into the parents'

responsibility to launch their children into adulthood. It reads: "Sons are a heritage from the Lord, children a reward from him. Like arrows in the hands of a warrior are sons born in ones' youth. Blessed is the man whose quiver is full of them." Calling children arrows is a telling metaphor. I (Shel) just watched the 2020 Olympic Games (held in Tokyo in 2021 because of Covid) and I was fascinated by the mechanical bows the athletes used in the archery competition. The bows had been made for accuracy. They had mechanical sighting devices and pulleys for drawing back the arrow. And the arrows, machine made, were all virtually identical. Even with all these improvements on the bow and arrow, not every archer hit the bulls-eye every time.

I work with Okiek/Dorobo hunters in Kenya. I've watched the men as they make arrows. First they choose shafts, often from an *olgilai* tree that is known for straight and strong branches. Then they hammer away at four-inch nails to create an arrowhead. They fletch the arrows with eagle feathers and tie them to the shaft with thin sinews. Lastly, they make a glue by chewing the stems of a succulent bush and then spitting the resulting tacky material to seal the arrows to the shaft. Even with all their efforts, the arrows aren't always perfectly straight. But a good bowman learns the tendency of the arrow to go right or left. With this knowledge, he can launch his arrow to hit the target.

I believe this is what Psalm 127 meant when it says that children are like arrows – all different from the others. A skilled warrior will know how to launch each unique arrow, just as we as parents should study and know our children so we can launch them into adulthood. 12 Tasks gives us a chance to launch our arrows.

Rites of Passage: An African Perspective

As a young boy growing up in Kenya, I (Shel) often hiked with my friends in the forest around Kijabe. I remember one day when we met some Kikuyu boys about our age – around 12 years old. After greeting them, they asked me a question

I couldn't answer. "Have you been 'cumcised?" I really didn't know what being 'cumcised even meant. My friend Billy Mackenzie was more mature in matters of the world and he knew what they were talking about. He told them we'd been circumcised. They wanted to know when we'd had this operation. When Billy told them it happened when we were babies, they laughed.

Apparently, they were part of a group that was about to go through the traditional Kikuyu coming of age ceremony, which included undergoing the cut of circumcision. It was a mark that showed they were moving from childhood to adulthood. How could we become men if we'd been circumcised as babies? We had no answer.

When I came back to Kenya as a missionary in 1981, I edited a Christian youth magazine called *Today in Africa*. We ran personal experience articles showing Kenyan Christians living out their faith in a changing world. One big issue was the traditional rite of passage to adulthood. In Kikuyu culture, both the boys and the girls around the age of 12 went through a time of teaching and acculturation, but the highlight of this period was a physical cut that had to be endured to prove they had left their childhood behind.

I read *Facing Mt Kenya*, a book by Jomo Kenyatta, Kenya's first president. He'd written it many years before to preserve a history of his Kikuyu people, including this important custom, which was under threat. Kenyatta explained how the older generation passed on information to this new age group on how to live and behave in their society. There was teaching on roles within marriage, proper sexual conduct and how to live within the community at large. For the young men, there were tests of physical endurance. Often there would be a cross country race. The winner would be esteemed and receive the honor of being a spokesman for their age group. Often they would have to run through a tunnel of older men who would beat their naked backs with stinging nettles.

After the circumcision operation, there was a period where

this age group learned more adult skills together – hunting, herding and more. In addition, the elders continued to pass on their collective knowledge. The young men would graduate into a period of time as warriors before going on to marriage and becoming junior elders themselves. The girls went through a similar rite of passage and passing on of knowledge. There was never any question among the Kikuyu as to when childhood was over.

By the 1980s many Kikuyu Christians had lost touch with the importance of giving their children a rite of passage. As a result, there was a booming number of teen pregnancies. As we studied this issue at *Today in Africa*, we realized that Kenya's youth were not receiving much teaching on sexual behavior or how to be good adults. Parents expected the church or the schools to teach their children. In the traditional rite of passage, this teaching was often done by grandparents and older relatives. Without traditional rites of passage ceremonies, any teaching by the church or schools on these issues was fairly ineffective.

Mwaura Njoroge, my co-editor, and I decided to write a novel about the lost rites of passage. Calling the book *Against the Traditions*, we planned the plot and characters and then wrote alternate chapters. We each edited each other's sections. This gave me an insight into the Kikuyu perspective, while Mwaura was often surprised at my western views. The setting for the book started back in the 1920s during the controversy between the church and the Kikuyu over traditional rites of passage, with the main character being a Kikuyu pastor who found himself caught in the middle between his new faith in Christ and his traditions. He opted to follow Christ and reject the traditions, but the book goes on to show the negative results when youth have no ceremonies around their rites of passage. The book ended with the current church leaders wondering if they could create an alternative rite of passage? We concluded with a short section on how a church could help the youth by creating alternative rites of passage.

We weren't the only ones sounding out this message, and now ARPs, as alternative rites of passage are often referred to, are a regular feature for churches in Kenya. They often sponsor what they call Circumcision Camps for their youth in the month of December – which was the traditional month for circumcision ceremonies in the past. The young boys and girls are gathered in different places and go through a week or more of Bible-based teaching and classes. This rite of passage provides the group the chance to learn with agemates. ARPs usually end with a graduation ceremony of some kind with parents and other relatives attending.

I have visited several of these camps. For a group of Kalenjin young men, they had all had their operation on the same day. Several men in the community had then taught the young men how to build a traditional house and they all moved in and stayed in the house together. They learned to hunt and trap small animals. They all wore similar clothing during the healing time. Various pastors provided teaching. When I stopped by, the young boys-cum-men each gave me a verse from the Bible which they had chosen to build their lives around.

At an even bigger camp for girls near Narok, they took over a school for a week. The girls had a week of teaching and prayers and crafts like beadwork. But they had no physical operation. At the end of the week, the girls all wore a beaded headband they had made.

(Many of these girls were Maasai or Dorobo, and in their traditional rite of passage, a girl who has gone through the ceremony wears a special headband made of metal chain strands). These new beaded headbands spelled out messages. Some said: Say no to FGM (FGM stands for female genital mutilation, a more modern name for female circumcision). Other headbands said: Say yes to girl child education. In both Maasai and Kikuyu traditional culture, after a girl went through this ceremony, she would be married soon after, often to an older man.

These girls and their parents were making a statement. They

wanted their girls to be adults, but they wanted them to go on with their education and marry a bit later in life. The ceremony ended with some pastors giving special prayers of blessing. I was selected to give one of the prayers. Then they served a large cake and *chai*, Kenya's sweet milky tea. It wasn't a traditional rite of passage. But it was a significant event in the lives of these girls – an alternative rite of passage.

Some years after I turned the management of *Today in Africa* magazine over to Mwaura Njoroge and others, I had more close encounters with rites of passage. We moved to Naivasha to work with the Okiek/Dorobo, a group of hunter gatherers in the highland forests of the Mau. We found that they continued to practice traditional circumcision ceremonies.

We had a young Dorobo man named Leboo who came to our seminars and decided to be a follower of Jesus. His father had passed away and he lived with other relatives. One day he came to me and asked if I'd be the sponsor for his circumcision. He was almost 18 and he had never gone through the ceremony. But without a father, the relatives had never had the money to pay for the celebration. Now it was almost shameful that he hadn't been circumcised. So would I help him? They could have the cut done at a nearby medical clinic.

After the operation, they'd have a special tea at his relatives' house. I agreed to help out. A few weeks before the operation, Leboo had asked me to buy him a watch. I had purchased a knock-off Casio brand wristwatch from a street vendor in Naivasha. On the day of the circumcision, I drove Leboo and his family members to the clinic. I stood behind him as the doctor at the clinic performed the surgery with local anesthetic. I then gave them a ride home and we drank *chai* and ate *chapatis* together as Leboo went to the back room to sleep.

About a week later Leboo came back to my house. He had healed and he wanted a new watch. I was glad he had healed, but I didn't want to buy him another watch. "I bought you a watch just a few weeks ago," I pointed out.

Leboo got a horrified look on his face. "I can't wear that

watch again. It was something I wore when I was a child. Now I'm a man, all the clothes I had were given to my younger relatives, including that watch. My relatives helped me buy a new set of clothes from the *mitumba* (the used clothes market), because it would be shameful for a young man to go back and wear the clothes of this childhood. So I need a new watch."

Even without all the traditional ceremonies, Leboo's circumcision marked the end of the childhood era and his movement into adulthood.

The Apostle Paul used circumcision as a picture of what happens when a person believes in Jesus. Colossians 2:11-12 says, "In him (Christ) you were also circumcised, in the putting off of the sinful nature, not with a circumcision done by the hands of men but with the circumcision done by Christ, having been buried with him in baptism and raised with him through your faith in the power of God, who raised him from the dead." Paul saw the circumcision ceremony as a powerful picture of Christ cutting off our sinful nature as we trust in him. He compared that to the ceremony of baptism, where new believers are symbolically buried in the water and then raised through their faith, just as God raised Jesus from the dead. Ceremonies are a powerful way of passing on truth.

The Dorobo people used the rite of passage circumcision ceremony as a lead-in to another ceremony called 'Passing on the Fire.' I stood shivering in the early morning chill on Mt Eburru in the early 1990s. I had just witnessed a young man's circumcision in a Dorobo village and the successful candidate now lay huddled behind the hut under a blanket. A group of older Dorobo men gathered and called the young man's agemates around. The old men pulled out an *olpiron* stick and a slab of cedar wood. Crouching down, one old man took the stick and inserted it into a small round hole in the cedar. Then he twirled the stick between the flattened palms of his hands. Soon smoke curled from the wood. He added tiny bits of tinder and blew until it glowed orange. Then he passed the nascent fire to the younger men.

The young men continued blowing on it. They gathered sticks and firewood and soon had a roaring fire. We stood around the fire, warming ourselves. Then the old men took out a calabash of honey wine, swigged it, then spat it into the fire as a blessing. Each of the old men then promised to pass on the knowledge and traditions of tribe to the next generation. The elders committed themselves to passing on the fire.

As parents, we realize our children will grow up into adults, even if we don't do anything to teach and encourage them along the way. But if we want them to grow up well, with a proper understanding of their personhood and how they fit into the fabric of the world around them, we need to commit ourselves to passing on the fire. And a good way to do that is by creating a rite of passage.

The Need for a Rite of Passage to Adulthood Today

Just a warning if those of faith do not consider this rite of passage seriously. David Murrow, in his book, *Why Men Hate Going to Church*, has tracked the spiritual habits of males and found that between the age of ten and twenty boys begin to try and drop out of church. Just when young men need the support of the faith community, they are trying to leave it. He sees that a large part of this is because the church doesn't enable them to move into their manhood. He is focusing primarily on the North American church, but this may have wider ramifications.

"Since the church is unwilling to initiate young men into manhood, they do it themselves. They subject their bodies to all sorts of abuse. They adopt a hypermasculine persona, expunging every trace of femininity. They endure humbling rites of passage: drugs, promiscuity, tattoos, foul language, drunkenness, reckless driving, and violent behavior, to ease their pain and prove their manliness at the same time. And they flee the church, because of its feminine ways and reputation as a place of safety.

"What about the 'good boys' who don't get into much trouble? Even they prefer manly things. They listen to music that glorifies violence, misogyny, and sex. They play savage video games and gravitate to brutal 'cage fighter'-type sports. They watch action movies replete with fights, explosions, and swaggering heroes. Even nerds know that girls go for guys with great skills – nanchuk skills, bowhunting skills...you get the picture.

"If Christians could just figure out a way to keep boys engaged in the church, everyone would win. Young men would enter adulthood with fewer addictions, diseases, injuries, and psychological scars. Society would benefit from lower crime rates. And the church would benefit from the vitality young men bring to an organization."[5]

Whether you agree with Murrow or not, it is worth your while to pay attention to his focus on the need for rites of passage.

Matthew Bruner, Director of Men of Valor Ranch in Northport, WA, in a blogpost titled "When Does a Boy Become a Man?" states: "Boys need men in their lives. Women obviously play a role that is irreplaceable in a boy's adolescent experience. However, there is something that can only be imparted from another man...something that despite all of men's weaknesses and flaws can only come through a male figure. It is for that reason that I look at our culture and challenge the parameters of responsible adulthood and the definition we have given for maturity and manhood. I suggest that we have lost our definition of manhood and thus lost the pathway to manhood. Young men need older men in their lives to establish various 'rite of passage' opportunities that would mark the defining moments of coming into manhood."[6]

While I have great hope for the adjustments being made by the next generation, I accept the caution of what navigating the transition to adulthood means for young men and women who have no guiding markers to ease them into maturity. I would easily incorporate young women into this reality in saying

5   David Murrow, Why Men Hate Going to Church, (Nelson: Nashville, TN: 2011), p. 183

6   Matthew Bruner, "When Does a Boy Become a Man?" Strugglingteens.com, May 2, 2007.

that every girl needs a mature woman to model the design and practices for whom God molded them to be.

This past winter, I (Jack) watched a new family from Latin America inch their way from their car up an icy ramp toward shelter in a church. A chilling wind seemed to reach inside their good clothing and create a sense of shock and confusion. The ground beneath their feet had always been a source of firmness and assurance. Now, things were as uncertain as if a major earthquake had moved everything.

Family life in our world is experiencing a similar shift. With broken families, blended families, single parent families and every imaginable combination of human beings labeled as family, it would be comforting to know for certain that scripture has a three-step plan to take our children from childhood to adulthood.

We may promise to the gathered family of God that we will raise our children in the fear and admonition of the Lord, but that still doesn't give us a blueprint to make it happen. Every parent faces the humble task of desperately depending on God's grace to translate biblical truth and principle into real life transformative relationships. And through it all, they must accept that the good work which God begins is a work which He alone can bring to completion.

3

12 Compelling Reasons to Walk with your Young Teen into Adulthood

Here are 12 compelling reasons for planning and guiding your child on the adventure of 12 Tasks.

1. You believe that healthy young adults matter to our future.

The health of our next generations and their successful transition to adulthood is critical to the future of our families, our communities, and, ultimately, our society. Children rarely develop into healthy adults without positive role models, a sense of purpose, and a path to follow.

2. You clearly see a growing crisis among our youth.

There is increasing confusion over self-identity as culture, media, education and government hold out never-before-seen options. Young men are performing worse than young women in school, taking longer to 'grow up' and accept responsibility, and generally holding off on the commitments of marriage and adulthood. Transitions will mean making pro-active choices which give our children a fighting chance. As parents, we cannot leave the task to others. We must take action. 12 Tasks provides a straightforward but powerful tool.

3. You recognize the crucial role of a parent or adult figure in helping a young teen transition into adulthood.

Let's be frank. The importance of 'Dad' and even 'Mom' is under heavy fire today. The media typically paints fathers who do stick around as out-of-touch, slobs, stupid, unfaithful and crude. But studies continue to show that kids who have engaged fathers or male role models are much more likely to succeed.

4. You understand that many cultures find markers to transmit their values and beliefs.

Cultures that last transmit their values and beliefs. The importance of a successful transition is a fundamental truth that enduring cultures have understood and prioritized throughout history. 12 Tasks is intentionally designed to reflect our multi-cultural society.

5. You are willing to invest time and energy into your own young teen's future.

The 12 Tasks are designed specifically for how youth learn best. They teach through hands-on activities, challenges and tangible actions. You and your son or daughter will be able to mark progress towards completion.

6. You want something tailored to your own young teen, which will bring out their strengths and giftings.

Each 12 Tasks will look different because your son or daughter is unique. You help your young teen identify their strengths, interests, and passions so they can increase their sense of who they are. Your son or daughter may actually be surprised to recognize some things that will shape their future direction.

7. You realize the importance of community in raising our next generations.

Doing 12 Tasks with a group of parents and young teens helps build positive connections to a community of role models so you do not have to do it alone any longer. This provides important accountability and encouragement when times get tough. 12 Tasks is flexible enough, however, that you can do it as a single family unit.

8. You want to build positive virtues and critical skill sets into your young teen.

Through 12 tasks your son or daughter will learn critical values like responsibility, hard work, teamwork, delayed gratification and skill sets like goal setting, planning and self-evaluation.

9. You want to encourage spiritual growth and development into the heart of your young teen.

We believe that Christian faith and a biblical perspective give your son or daughter a strong foundation for meeting the challenges of teenage life. We encourage you to transmit your faith and values as part of the 12 Tasks.

10. You recognize that you are an ordinary adult with something to share and something to learn with your young teen.

12 Tasks is designed with the average parent in mind. You don't have to be Mr. or Mrs. Outdoors, Mr. or Mrs. Builder, Mr. or Mrs. Athletic or Mr. or Mrs. Intellectual to make a difference in the life of your son or daughter. In fact, prepare to check your ego at the door. Our experience is that at times this journey can be very humbling—and that is a good thing!

11. You want to encourage parents and young teens to care for others through shared experiences.

12 Tasks is not easy and this means that your son or daughter will have an accomplishment that they can look back on as a young person when they face future challenges. It also gives them positive and compelling stories they can share with their peers.

12. You enjoy sharing ideas and experiences with others who are in the same stage of life.

We strongly advocate for group tasks that focus on serving others. Our society is so me-focused and our sons and daughters are inundated with the view that their own pleasure and happiness is most important. There is nothing like checking out of your comfort zone and taking a step into someone else's shoes.

If those aren't compelling enough, then listen to this from my son, Richard, who completed his 12 Tasks and recently took his own son, Jordan, through the 12 Tasks.

Why the 12 Tasks were so Important to Me

From Richard Taylor (son of Jack and Gayle and father of Jordan, Anderson, Micah and Miriam)

For me, the power of the 12 Tasks was not as much in the specific tasks, but rather in the principles behind them, and the process I went through to accomplish them.

Relevance

My parents put a lot of thought into choosing tasks that were appropriate for me. Some tasks leveraged strengths in writing, critical thinking and relationship building. Other tasks helped me to confront areas where I lacked confidence, such as my mechanical abilities and my athletic skills. Together, the tasks attempted to build qualities like a strong work ethic, discipline, spiritual commitment, compassion for others, cultural understanding and leadership into my life. Eighteen years later I can see clearer how appropriate the tasks were.

Impact

My tasks were not 'make work' projects. Each one was thoughtfully designed to have an intentional impact on my life. Reading through the Bible in a year helped provide a strong spiritual foundation for my transition to manhood and encouraged me to embrace my faith as my own. Building a tree fort gave me confidence that with hard work and dedication I could succeed where I was not naturally gifted. Writing a 70-page book (once I started I couldn't stop) solidified my love for the written word. My research article on the hardest part about growing up made me realize I was not alone in the challenges of teenage life.

Affirmation

Affirmation is so important for a boy transitioning to manhood. I needed the security that my parents loved me unconditionally but they also recognized I was growing up and were prepared to give me a much greater level of trust and responsibility. Affirmation had a huge role in the 12 Tasks. Not everything went smoothly and there were days I was unmotivated. My parent's encouragement and belief were huge. I will never forget the celebration we had upon completing the tasks. My parents invited adults who had influence in my life to speak words of encouragement and vision for the future.

Relationship

12 Tasks deepened my relationship with my father. They provided a natural way for my Dad to relate with me that moved our relationship closer into the realm of mutual respect and friendship. The tasks we did together – like climbing Mt. Kenya and building a tree fort (something I later realized he felt equally incompetent about) – were the most meaningful to me. They only become more meaningful in retrospect and have a great influence as I think about how to build relationships with my three boys.

Flexibility

My parents gave me some choice in the selection of tasks. They came up with 16 possible tasks and I chose the 12 I wanted to accomplish. Perhaps even more important, they did not see this list as completely sacrosanct and they ended up rewarding me with a bonus task during a time when they saw me standing up against prejudice. This was a quality they knew would be extremely important in my adult life and I still have the signed certificate from my father sharing why he was proud of me.

Trust

An inherent message I received from my parents (and especially my Dad) during 12 Tasks was that they trusted me. I cannot overstate the importance of this dynamic for a boy transitioning to manhood. The presence of trust as a boy grows older will greatly ease his transition. Its absence will be a considerable roadblock and will either lead to increasing animosity or unhealthy reliance. I will never forget a conversation I had with my Dad at age 16 when I had been deceitful about activities I was doing with my friends. He said he wanted to trust me and my actions were breaking down that trust. That short conversation was huge in my transition to manhood.

The health of our youth is critical to the future of our families, our communities and ultimately—our entire society. This is a fundamental truth that most enduring cultures have understood throughout history.

Unfortunately, we face a near crisis of adulthood in western society. Today broken families, floundering youth, and directionless young adults are common. On average, boys are doing worse in school than girls, are more likely to drop out of high school and less likely to graduate from university. Many young men are unmotivated, lack tangible goals for the future, and have a poor relationship (if any relationship at all) with their dad.

Few dads take the time to meaningfully engage their sons and to intentionally walk alongside them and model what it means to be a man. Peers, video games and the mass media fill the void as boys transfer their hopes and ambitions into the isolation of an increasingly virtual world.

In *What Makes A Man? (12 Promises That Will Change*

Your Life) Gary Smalley and John Trent focus on the Promises You Make to Your Family.[7] They've identified assertiveness, self-confidence, independence and self-control as foundational to masculinity with the fifth trait being stability. If a father hopes to see these in his son, they should first be anchored in himself. Fathers need to hug their daughters as studies show that healthy affection between parents and daughters keeps them feeling safe and satisfied at home longer. Our culture is shifting so quickly under the feet of our children that stability at home is essential for them as they dare to step away.

While the 12 Tasks are an excellent tool for parents to lead their son or daughter to adulthood, it can be especially useful for a Father and Son to successfully navigate the journey from Boy to Man. This transformative life transition cannot be assumed. Fathers have a critical and proactive role in their son's life. In recognition of this important challenge, 12 Tasks can help you as a father work together with your son to proactively design a year of testing, initiation and affirmation.

The beauty of the 12 Tasks is not only in what is accomplished over a one-year period as your son or daughter strive to embrace the challenges that have been set. The beauty is in the bonding and relationship building that is part of the process of walking your children into adulthood. During this year, other mentors may be drawn into the process so that a strong community of positive role models are linked to the ongoing success and well-being of your child becoming an adult – male role models for your son and female role models for your daughter.

It is my firm belief that God placed us in a world of relationships to help us to grow deeper in our awareness of who we are and what we are called to do here. In marriage, parents discover issues of character at a deeper level than they sometimes care to know. Yet, in a committed and affirming

---

7   McCartney, Bill, What Makes A Man? (NavPress: Colorado Springs, 1992), pp. 83-94.

relationship like this, husband and wife are free to explore, discover and deal with flaws, then build on the strengths.

With the arrival of children, the depths of discovery for parents go deeper still. They discover levels of tenderness, gentleness, frustration and impatience deeper than they believe possible. They learn sacrifice and make choices which aren't always in their best immediate interests. They gain perspective on a world bigger than themselves.

Interacting with growing children on the verge of adulthood will take you another step into self-discovery. For fathers, it is good to be aware that sometimes the son can be a 'young bull' moving toward independence away from (at times against) the 'old bull.' Affirming independence without overreacting at immature attempts at adulthood is an important skill for parents in releasing their children to grow up.

Sometimes, some intentional guidance is needed. I remember in 2011, watching the television in disbelief. My disappointment at losing game 7 of the Stanley Cup Finals was quickly eclipsed by the scene of angry Vancouver Canucks fans starting a riot, setting fire to cars, destroying property, and defying the police. Around them were crowds of onlookers taking pictures and videos with mobile phones, making it nearly impossible for the undermanned police to intervene.

My immediate thought was that the professional protestors and anarchists had once again taken advantage of a big event to cause chaos. This is what happened prior to the 2010 Winter Olympics. But the pictures on the screen didn't seem to fit that scenario. The rioters were, overwhelmingly, young men in their late teens and early twenties, all wearing Canucks' jerseys. They looked exactly like the young men I see every day near my neighborhood.

In the aftermath of the Vancouver riots, it became clear that the typical profile of a rioter was actually a middle-class male from the suburbs. One rioter who turned himself in was the son of a doctor and a decorated water polo player. For me, the iconic photo of the riots was this clean cut young man – with his bleach blond hair – trying to light a gasoline soaked rag stuffed into the tank of a police cruiser.

Who are these boys and what happened to them?

It was tempting to write this off as an isolated and unfortunate incident, the fatal combination of a hyped up and bitterly disappointed crowd, too much alcohol, and way too much testosterone. But I could not shake the feeling that it was actually the result of something bigger, that it was another symptom of a growing number of boys and young men (and even young women) who are not effectively making the transition to adulthood.

Richard Rohr says: "When a culture no longer initiates its males into the proper carrying of power, we can assume they will almost always abuse it or avoid it, both of which are a loss to the community."[8]

Even before him, the Greek philosopher, Aristotle is said to have remarked that "to be a competent student of what is right and just; one must first have learned discipline and received a proper upbringing in moral conduct. A man with this background has acquired the foundations of life. One who has not may one day be called useless."

There are plenty of books and articles analyzing the crisis of manhood, or personhood, and why boys are falling behind in school and everything else associated with that. This book is designed to be deeply personal and deeply practical to give you a tool you can use to help your child make the successful transition to adulthood.

Here is a quick psychological overview of the stages of life. 12 Tasks focuses most significantly on Stage 5 (Identity Formation). The need for this could be connected to research on 'Emerging Adulthood' that shows how today's young people are walking through this developmental stage and 'growing up' much later.

---

8 Richard Rohr, From Wild Man to Wise Man: Reflections on Male Spirituality

Psychological Overview of The Stages of Life — Review the psychological stages that your child has gone through as outlined below and evaluate whether there has been a healthy completion of that stage. How well have you truly observed your child?

Parents have become increasingly aware of the week by week and month by month physical and behavioral development of their child without necessarily noticing the overall psychosocial transitions underway. Erik Erikson's careful observation of humans within their cultural framework has helped him provide a descriptive overview as a tool to analyze emotional and social growth. He postulates eight stages with stages 5-8 being especially significant for the 12 Tasks. Each stage has a positive and negative tension, which must be worked through. The successful completion of one stage allows an individual to progress well into the following stage. An unsuccessful experience at any level results in negative complications when moving to the following stage. Here are the stages and the typical ages where the tension is faced.

1 **Trust vs. Mistrust (0-18 months)**. If needs are consistently, predictably and reliably met, then a sense of trust will yield a virtue of hope. A sense of attachment to a stable adult is crucial in this phase. How did your child do with their attachment and trust?

2 **Autonomy vs. Shame and Doubt (18 months-3 years)**. If independence and a personal control of physical abilities is encouraged and supported, then a sense of autonomy will lead to the virtue of will, resulting in confidence and security. How did your child do with the sense of autonomy, confidence and security during these early years?

3 **Initiative vs. Guilt (3-4 years)**. Regular interaction with other children, where play and interpersonal skills

are initiated, will confirm a security to lead others, to ask questions and to make personal decisions resulting in affirmed purpose. How did your child do in their interaction with others, their initiation of play and relationship and in their asking of questions and decision making?

4 Industry (Competence) vs. Inferiority (5-12 years). School skills gain importance, resulting in a transfer of influence to teachers and peers. Approval is sought through demonstrated competencies valued by society so that self-esteem is established and the virtue of competence is gained. How well did your child do in their demonstrated competencies gained at school, community groups and church?

5 Identity vs. Role Confusion (12-18 years). A search for personal identity through exploring values, beliefs and goals marks the transition toward adulthood. The desire to fit into society becomes stronger; exploring roles and opportunities increases; a re-examination of identity surfaces - sexual, social, and career identity is negotiated and confirmed. A successful navigation of these years results in the virtue of fidelity where the individual can accept others and commit to others.

Phase 5 is the place where we need to focus on since an identity crisis or role confusion will leave the young teen drifting and exploring options which could leave them vulnerable to persuasive peers or adults who might take advantage of their exploration. Pressure in one direction or another can result in resistance and choices, which create regrets for parent and teen. Establishing a strong sense of self-identity here will allow the teen to prepare for the intimacy required in adult years.

Still to come: Maybe you can consider how well you or your parents have done in these areas?

6 Intimacy vs. Isolation (18-40 years). This stage focuses on the forming of loving relationships and commitment with others. Parents of young teens may be emerging from their work in this area and their successful completion will help them in mentoring. The virtue of love is a result of successful work in this phase.

7 Generativity vs. Stagnation (40-65 years). During this seventh stage, which will cover most participating parents and grandparents, we see the importance of establishing your mark on someone or something that will outlast you. Society is enriched as we nurture children, mentor others and become involved in community. Success here is not only good for the next generations but also for us who recognize the value of what we leave behind. The virtue here is about care.

8 Integrity vs. Despair (65+years). Grandparents and great grandparents may also have a role to play in adding words of wisdom and celebration. They may even have skills to pass on. This phase is about contemplating accomplishments, and what better way than to impact and influence the youngest generations. The virtue in this phase is called wisdom.

We all need security, significance and the feeling of being special, seen, loved and wanted. Ideally, we parent in such a way that our child gains these. Notice if your son or daughter is searching for something that doesn't seem to be anchored yet. Everyone will act out in ways to get their needs met if there is still an unhealed wound. We are people often driven by fear, guilt, shame or anger due to this wounding and it is important that we deal with our own issues so we don't project our journey into the life of our child. As you take this journey to honestly see your son or daughter, you may also get a glimpse of yourself. Don't back away from the mirror.

"While it's true that the brain reaches over 90% of its

structural size by the sixth year of a child's life, we now know that the brain undergoes dramatic and essential internal development in the years leading up to and throughout adolescence."[9]

---

9   Clark, Ibid, p. 16

PART 2

PLANNING THE 12 TASKS

Approaching our Sons and Daughters

You may be convinced that doing 12 Tasks together will make a difference for you and your son or daughter. But will they feel the same way?

Perhaps you are one of those blessed parents whose child is up for any new challenge. If you have a good relationship already and know your son or daughter will be receptive, then you may be able to quickly introduce the concept and get their feedback.

Francine and Harry had twin daughters approaching their twelfth year and started looking for ways to celebrate. They read an article by Jack in a local Christian newspaper featuring the 12 Tasks and contacted him to find out more. That conversation led to their investment in co-parenting their daughters through a coming-of-age series of tasks and a celebration at the end. They approached their daughters by suggesting that in many cultures children who approached their twelfth and thirteenth years were given opportunities to prove they were ready for more privileges and responsibilities as emerging adults. The girls accepted the process as part of their growing up and apart from some resistance part way through the year all went well.

There is, however, a good chance they will be resistant at first, especially if there is strain in your relationship, if they feel that you are treating them like a project or if they are struggling with issues of self-worth.

If this is the case, we encourage you not to start with pushing 12 Tasks, but give them the time they need and talk with them in a non-threatening environment. Is there something you enjoy doing together, like fishing, hiking or going to a sporting match? Work in the time to ask your son or daughter about your relationship and how they are feeling about the future. Identify things they talk about that may allow you the room to introduce 12 Tasks. Share some stories of young adults they know and admire who have had an intentional transition to adulthood. Give them Shel's book *Test of the Tribal Challenge*, which features a fictional account of the 12 Tasks, and then ask if they would like their own challenge.

Mel and Jane received a text from their church's family pastor sharing his interest in taking his son through a guided 12 Tasks. There were five boys in the same age range and he wondered if any of the other parents might be interested. They showed the text to their son Gavin who shrugged. They didn't push him and replied to the family pastor that it didn't look like Gavin was ready for this. The next week Gavin asked what kind of tasks he might have to do. By not pushing too hard they allowed for Gavin to approach the family pastor's son at youth group to find out what this was all about. Three of the five boys joined their fathers in supporting each other through the 12 Tasks.

Richard had stayed in contact with many of his college friends who, like him, had boys reaching their transition into being teens. He asked his dad, Jack, for materials on the 12 Tasks and spun his own story of going through the 12 Tasks. Richard is a great salesman and a class one story-teller so was able to draw interest from several of these fathers immediately. Not all followed through and not all completed the tasks as they tried to persevere in the middle of a pandemic with its own challenges. Those who did engage gained a new appreciation for the struggle to come alongside their sons at a busy time of life. The successful fathers seemed to try to retell Richard's stories and put out the idea to their sons. Enthusiasm and investment are helpful but solid parenting relationships seem crucial as a foundation first.

Gina was a single mom with sons two years apart. She

wondered if both the boys could do it together with help from one of the men in her community. She approached her brother with some of the literature on 12 Tasks. He felt the investment of time might be too much. She approached a coach, a youth pastor and her own uncle. None of them seemed enthused at the length of commitment involved. She was ready to give up when her brother suggested a friend who also had a son the same age. The brother set up a meeting for the two parents and attended to avoid wrong impressions. All three boys were invited to a second meeting so they could meet, ask questions, address concerns, and think up ideas on how to move forward. Gina's brother stayed more engaged than she had hoped and was able to give the celebration speech for the boys at the end.

Whatever your approach, make sure your son or daughter is part of the decision to do 12 Tasks from the very beginning, and is committed to doing them, or you will risk alienating or discouraging them. I (Jack) didn't do as well in inviting my daughters into ownership of the 12 Tasks of Womanhood and as a result, some of the tasks met with more resistance than I faced with Richard. Gayle and I approached our daughters Michelle and Laura once Richard had finished his tasks. We assumed that having an older sibling set the standard would draw our daughters into the process of 12 Tasks easily. It did help to normalize the 12 Tasks for those who came after Richard, but I let my own enthusiasm for the challenge override their desire to engage. I feel we could have done better in approaching our daughters.

If a parent, relative, family friend or grandparent can tell their stories of how they came of age and if the 12 Tasks were part of the transition it will prove more inviting for the son or daughter who is ready to prove themselves. Each parent knows what draws their child into something and what repels them. Showing individual sensitivity to challenge and draw out your child's character will help set out a successful process. This is a significant investment into the life of a child but it will be transformational and potentially eternal in its fruit.

I (Jack) have completed ten novels and one of the realities in the stories is that the protagonist, the hero, the main character, goes on an adventure that matters. Youth are exposed to heroes in all their media contact and it would be wise for parents to consider changing their role from being the hero to their child to being the guide in their child's hero's journey. If your son or daughter is at the center of the adventure, with hints and encouragement to solve the major issue of becoming an adult, then it may make a crucial difference.

Generational Differences

It is important to understand our children's generation and how they relate to other generations as we approach our sons and daughters about completing 12 Tasks.

At the time we began writing this manuscript there were four generations of Taylors in our lineage now active on the planet. My own father, Charles, was in his nineties and is sometimes labeled as being in the traditionalist or builder generation. I, Jack, am clearly planted in the middle of the Baby Boomers. Richard lives and breathes the life of the Gen Xers, and his sons are living in the Gen Zers.

How we work, view our world, and influence those around us, is not only a matter of culture and personality. It is also a matter of generation and history. We are motivated differently and we look for different goals and rewards along the way. All this may impact the way you frame your tasks.

My father's generation built their neighborhoods and communities with loyalty and dedication. It was their duty as they pioneered the way. They would often work in the same line of work for most of their life. These men faithfully beat the path through the wilderness, fought major battles, and sacrificed for their families. Their reward was job security, strong relationships and a good pension. Now is the time to share life experiences, relationship networks, and the legacy that will establish their identity. They need to know they will not be forgotten.

My generation still usually sees work as a responsibility

where long hours and lengthy years are justified and where the reward is fulfilled in the need to be needed. Economic uncertainty may mean job changes and long-term benefits are becoming uncertain. We loyally and ambitiously follow the path set out for us but broaden it and manage it so that others behind us can easily find the way. We want to know we are still valued and needed and look for the tangible perks to show this.

Richard's generation often sees work as a difficult challenge that may only be one of several careers they pursue in a lifetime of work. Many of those eager to get ahead will stick with the job as long as there is sufficient freedom for growth and expression. They are willing to follow the path set down for them as long as they are also free to explore other options along the way. With so much uncertainty around them, this group feels less tied down to one certain pathway. They value freedom and independence and need frequent outside affirmation to keep them travelling in the same direction.

Those born in the 1990s or later often want to set their own journey and craft their own adventure. Established paths before them seem to hold no sense of life or daring. They yearn to rebreathe the pioneering spirit of their great-grandparents. This generation wants a say and a chance to make a difference. Personal gratification is important. They have little confidence, want instant gratification and need constant positive feedback, meaningful work and significant flexibility. Trusting them to use their technological skills to accomplish what is needed is almost essential.

Culture guru, Tim Elmore, in his book *Generation Z Unfiltered*[10], says that partnering with our children is more important than ever. He says this generation is more private with information because of what they have witnessed happening to millennials on social media but they also may focus their photos or videos and comments on vanishing platforms like Snapchat, Instagram, or Calculator% where content can be hidden from parents or other prying eyes.

---

10   Tim Elmore, Generation Z Unfiltered, (Poet Gardner: Atlanta, GA, 2019), pp. 25-32

This generation is also more anxious. More information has been generated in the past two years (2020-2021) than in all human history before combined. World tragedies are constantly streamed into their consciousness through news sources. They've grown up with Covid, Zoom, Netflix, Hulu, Instagram, TikTok, Reddit, Amazon Prime, Youtube, Google, Siri and Alexis filling their down times. They're dealing with intersectionality, woke culture, transgenderism, racism, identity politics, environmentalism, and many more issues where their every word and action is dissected and analyzed. They feel responsible as the scapegoats for much of what is happening.

Elmore says this generation is also restless, with 11 percent being diagnosed with ADHD. Identity is evolving from what is happening online rather than from family or community groups. He says "what is concerning to me is their lack of congruency. I believe we as humans are at our best when we have a sense of integrity and congruency about ourselves – when we're not duplicitous."[11] These kids are Tech Savvy, spending nine or more hours a day on screens. Many of their relationships are developed online. They are entrepreneurial which may be an advantage with the tasks you choose. Equality has become a top issue and they are growing up believing that they can change the world.

The challenge in dealing with the changes in the next generations is that our role as parents with that generation may also be changing so that we may be in uncharted territory. Elmore says that parenting now is not about control but about staying connected so you can "guide them into self-awareness, self-management, social awareness, relationship management and responsible decision-making." Parents generally have become consumed with "safety, self-esteem and success of Generation Z kids."

The search for identity is a real issue in a world confused about how to distinguish ourselves among billions of others. There are plenty of personalities calling on our youth to

---

11   Elmore, Generation Z Unfiltered, p. 28

become like them. Where you anchor that identity can make all the difference in how you form your tasks. Are we who we are because of our birthplace, race, tribe, religion, sexuality, gender, age, social status, wealth, political persuasion, education, addiction, social cause, skin color, birth order, language, influence on social media or some other marker? Perhaps engagement with a cause that matters to them might be an anchor point in drawing them into the task of becoming someone unique worth following. Use their interest in social media to help broadcast what they are doing and thus set up an informal accountability system.

As you approach your daughter or son, keep in mind these ten commandments that Kevin Lehman has constructed for parents as they interact with their children. While this list has a focus on younger children, it can help parents create a family culture that will still come into play as your offspring nears their teen years.

- My hands are small; please don't expect perfection whenever I make a bed, draw a picture, or throw a ball.
- My legs are short; slow down so that I can keep up with you.
- My eyes have not seen the world as yours have; let me explore it safely; don't restrict me unnecessarily.
- Housework will always be there; I'm little only for a short time. Take time to explain things to me about this wonderful world, and do so willingly.
- My feelings are tender; don't nag me all day long (you would not want to be nagged for your inquisitiveness). Treat me as you would like to be treated.
- I am a special gift from God; treasure me as God intended you to do – holding me accountable for my actions, giving me guidelines to live by, and disciplining me in a loving manner.
- I need your encouragement (but not your empty praise) to grow. Go easy on the criticism; remember, you can criticize the things I do without criticizing me.
- Give me the freedom to make decisions concerning

myself. Permit me to fail, so that I can learn from my mistakes. Then someday I'll be prepared to make the decisions life will require of me.

- Don't do things over for me; that makes me feel my efforts didn't measure up to your expectations. I know it's hard, but don't compare me with my brother or my sister.
- Don't be afraid to leave for a weekend together. Kids need vacations from parents, and parents need vacations from kids. Besides, it's a great way to show us kids that your marriage is something special.
- Take me to Sunday School and church regularly, setting a good example for me to follow. I enjoy learning more about God.[12]

Finally, as you approach your budding teen about doing 12 Tasks, take note of Tim Elmore's list of paradoxes for this new generation as they grow up in uncertain times.[13]

- They are independent yet dependent on parents.
- They are trendy yet traditional in practices.
- They are both often alone yet never alone.
- They have it so good yet have it so difficult.
- They experience virtually no dramatic moments yet feel so much drama.
- They are cognitively advanced yet emotionally behind.
- Their life is both authentic and artificial.
- Their world is easy but very hard.

"Because of the progressive remodeling of the brain during this period, the teen years can be an amazing season of cultivating creativity, self-awareness, and passion for things that really matter."[14]

---

12   Kevin Lehman, quoted in Dear Abby Independent Press Telegram, January 12, 1981.

13   Elmore, p. 31.

14   Clark, p. 13

5

Assessing your Son or Daughter

The better you know your son or daughter, where they are at, and what challenges they will likely face in their transition to adulthood, the more likely it is that you will design tasks that are relevant and make a lasting difference in their life.

Anyone who knows me (Jack) understands that I am immensely proud of my children. My son, specifically, has an inborn intensity which drives him. He is the firstborn of two firstborns and it shows. My son's expectations for himself are high and his frustrations run deep when he falls short. It has always been this way – from even before the time he was a grade two boy trying to prove himself on the soccer field with the grade six boys. That year he read the Chronicles of Narnia through seven times. He memorized a huge number of verses for his Sunday School program. He explored his world like a pioneer possessed.

Choosing tasks for Richard wasn't only about finding something to keep him busy. Choosing tasks involved understanding his character strengths and weaknesses, his existing skills set and the gaps in that skill set, and it involved some awareness of the demands from the world in which he would take his place as a man. A father brings that overarching perspective of life, experience and understanding to help his son take some significant steps toward holistic interdependence in his world.

But even a father can only see so much. It is more important for the son to build a confidence that his father believes in him and will be there for him whenever possible. The details of the tasks are not as crucial as the heart connection that is happening in your relationship along the way.

If you need some help to think about who your son or daughter is, feel free to use our simple assessment tool **(Knowing Your Son or Daughter)**. It helps you to get a snapshot of where they are at in 20 different areas which are important to their long-term development. Think of the assessment as the raw data you can use to choose 12 Tasks. It will help you gain a clearer picture of your child's strengths, natural abilities, weaknesses and areas for growth.

Knowing Your Son or Daughter

Below are 20 different categories you might consider when creating tasks for your son or daughter. If 20 categories seems daunting, you can simplify it by choosing those categories that are most closely linked to the tasks you are considering.

STEPS:
1. Choose a category from the chart below which you might consider for a task. Add others if you think of them.
2. Look at the five statements listed under that category in the next section.
3. Mark off whether each statement is never true, occasionally true, often true, or always true for your son or daughter. Include your child as much as possible as you complete the grid so he or she takes ownership of this with you.
4. Transfer this information onto the chart below.
5. Consider the information when you plan your tasks.

Choose a category *– the statements for each will help you understand better what is being considered in this area.*

Our suggestion is that you choose four demonstrated areas of strength and create tasks that will make these areas even more pronounced. Choose four less developed areas and create tasks that will develop a more well-rounded young person. Choose four tasks that will help develop your relationship together – two in which you can pass on your special skills and two in which you can learn skills together. By combining several of these categories into single tasks you can make this even more enriching and challenging for both of you. Remember the biblical directive not to exasperate your son (Ephesians 6:4) and plan accordingly.

Fill in one square for each statement that is usually or always true for your son or daughter at this time of life. [Work through the categories and their statements and then return here].

Spiritual					
Personal					
Financial					
Physical					
Sexual					
Moral					
Ethical					
Global					
Relational					
Social					
Verbal					
Character					
Biblical					
Mechanical					
Musical					
Creative					
Literary					
Intuitive					
Compassion					
Teachable					

The following pages contain the specifics you will be looking for.

Statements: check off the level which is true for your son or daughter. Mentally insert their name in the blank. Four or five statements in the same category at level 3 or 4 would indicate a strength for your son or daughter. This is an important time for honest reflection and perhaps conversation with your son or daughter. If you think of a phrase that better captures the essence of your son or daughter in one particular area, and you know this would help you formulate a task for your son or daughter, feel free to substitute your phrase for one of the ones listed. Or add it if that works better. This is a guideline to help you.

1 = Never True 2 = Occasionally True 3 = Usually True 4 = Always True

Spiritual:

	1.	2.	3.	4.
a.				
b.				
c.				
d.				
e.				

a._____ prays freely and comfortably (alone, in a group)
b._____ loves to read the Bible
c._____ studies and memorizes Scripture
d._____ adjusts life to what is read in the Bible
e._____ is a positive influence on peers

Personal:

	1.	2.	3.	4.
a.				
b.				
c.				
d.				
e.				

    a._____ treats others with dignity and respect
    b._____ practices self-control consistently
    c._____ thinks through consequences for all actions
    d._____ is worthy of trust and is respected by adults
    e._____ is respectful of and considerate toward authority

Financial:

	1.	2.	3.	4.
a.				
b.				
c.				
d.				
e.				

    a._____ knows how to save money wisely
    b._____ understands the importance of tithing
    c._____ is ready to earn money with good work
    d._____ spends money wisely
    e._____ is learning to be generous with others

Physical:

	1.	2.	3.	4.
a.				
b.				
c.				
d.				
e.				

a._____ lives an active lifestyle on a regular basis
b._____ has learned to value healthy eating
c._____ gets a good balance of sleep and exercise
d._____ refrains from engaging in senseless risky behavior
e._____ is not afraid to be challenged physically

Sexual:

	1.	2.	3.	4.
a.				
b.				
c.				
d.				
e.				

a._____ treats his/her own body with dignity and respect
b._____ practices self-control consistently
c._____ thinks through consequences for his/her actions
d._____ is worthy of trust and is respected by adults
e._____ speaks respectfully to/about the opposite sex

Moral:

	1.	2.	3.	4.
a.				
b.				
c.				
d.				
e.				

    a._____ has a strong sense of right and wrong
    b._____ understands the standards we set in our home
    c._____ makes good decisions even when I'm not around
    d._____ is an influence for good on his/her peers
    e._____ avoids the extremes of legalism and apathy

Ethical:

	1.	2.	3.	4.
a.				
b.				
c.				
d.				
e.				

    a._____ has a strong sense of justice and fairness
    b._____ has a clear understanding of compassion
    c._____ accepts people without always accepting behavior
    d._____ is interested in understanding why things are right
    e._____ easily sees the difference between right and wrong

Global:

	1.	2.	3.	4.
a.				
b.				
c.				
d.				
e.				

a._____ is interested in what is happening in our world
b._____ connects well with people from other nations
c._____ has a desire to travel and explore
d._____ questions and researches about global causes
e._____ has clear opinions on international news stories

Relational:

	1.	2.	3.	4.
a.				
b.				
c.				
d.				
e.				

a._____ treats others with dignity and respect
b._____ builds relationships with others easily
c._____ is gracious and generous with others
d._____ knows how to apologize when wrong
e._____ is able to sort through conflicts thoughtfully

Social:

	1.	2.	3.	4.
a.				
b.				
c.				
d.				
e.				

    a._____ would rather be with people than be alone
    b._____ seems to gain energy from being with others
    c._____ is comfortable with almost any group
    d._____ influences others in groups in positive ways
    e._____ finds it easy to make friends wherever

Verbal:

	1.	2.	3.	4.
a.				
b.				
c.				
d.				
e.				

    a._____ is very gifted with vocabulary
    b._____ spends a lot of time talking with others
    c._____ is able to motivate others with words
    d._____ tells stories and happenings easily
    e._____ communicates thoughts clearly

Character:

	1.	2.	3.	4.
a.				
b.				
c.				
d.				
e.				

a._____ is respected by peers and adults alike
b._____ demonstrates the fruit of the spirit (Gal. 5:22-23)
c._____ lives out a humility and gentleness with others
d._____ responds appropriately to authority figures
e._____ embraces a balance of truth and grace in life

Biblical:

	1.	2.	3.	4.
a.				
b.				
c.				
d.				
e.				

a._____ has a strong desire for reading the Bible
b._____ is willing to memorize and recite Scripture verses
c._____ has a strong understanding of the Bible message
d._____ shares biblical truth with others freely
e._____ is able to apply truth to a personal situation

Mechanical:

	1.	2.	3.	4.
a.				
b.				
c.				
d.				
e.				

a._____ is curious about how physical things work
b._____ readily assembles and disassembles things
c._____ understands how to fix the broken
d._____ is creative in constructing what is missing
e._____ is able to design new models of mechanisms

Musical:

	1.	2.	3.	4.
a.				
b.				
c.				
d.				
e.				

a._____ responds attentively to songs with interest
b._____ expresses desire to learn and play instruments
c._____ loves to sing songs that have been shared
d._____ gravitates toward those with talents in music
e._____ demonstrates ability in tone, pitch, range of voice

Creative:

	1.	2.	3.	4.
a.				
b.				
c.				
d.				
e.				

    a._____ tends to try to do most things in unique ways
    b._____ loves to use their imagination in play
    c._____ is drawn toward beauty and diverse art
    d._____ has an ability to capture what they see
    e._____ uses hands and mind to create new things

Literary:

	1.	2.	3.	4.
a.				
b.				
c.				
d.				
e.				

    a._____ devours books, stories and the written word
    b._____ writes, spells and shares ideas easily
    c._____ understands deep thought and theory
    d._____ gravitates toward and appreciates classical works
    e._____ enjoys and writes poetry, fiction and letters easily

Intuitive:

	1.	2.	3.	4.
a.				
b.				
c.				
d.				
e.				

    a._____ can guess the meaning of a word by looking at it
    b._____ has a strong sense of what is happening
    c._____ is aware of feelings and inner thoughts
    d._____ has a strong tendency toward optimism
    e._____ tends to easily build trust with others

Compassion:

	1.	2.	3.	4.
a.				
b.				
c.				
d.				
e.				

    a._____ tends to initiate acts of care for others
    b._____has others remark how kind and thoughtful they are
    c._____ has a sensitivity to pets or people who struggle
    d._____ tends to give others the benefit of the doubt
    e._____ voluntarily feels with and for others

Teachable:

	1.	2.	3.	4.
a.				
b.				
c.				
d.				
e.				

    a._____ reaches out to those who know more
    b._____ listens eagerly and responds immediately
    c._____ isn't paralyzed by failure but tries again
    d._____ accepts correction and learns quickly to adjust
    e._____ has a humble and receptive spirit to instruction

These are samples of traits and categories you can use in assessment. Take your time and don't be overly expectant on assuming your son or daughter should be higher in certain categories. Every child is a unique gift from the Creator and your task is to discern that blend of being which God has already knit together to accomplish the tasks he has designed and desired. If it helps, find another trusted individual who can help you clarify the strengths and growth areas for your son or daughter.

Finding Strengths

Tom Rath, in his book *Strengths Finder 2.0*, identifies Strength as the ability to consistently provide near-perfect performance [p.20]. His formula for determining strength is to first identify a talent (a natural way of thinking, feeling or behaving) and multiplying it by investment (time spent practicing, developing your skills and building your knowledge base). I've included brief definitions of the strengths as a help in your analysis.

Perhaps the following list will help you understand your

own strengths as well as your son's or daughter's. If you want more information, I encourage you to check out the resource. I include the list because sometimes we tend to view traits which are different than ours as growth areas rather than strengths. The purpose of the 12 Tasks is to encourage your son or daughter to become who God designed them to be rather than what you want them to be.

The talents Rath has defined from assessing millions of interviews include the following:

Achiever – Hard worker with extra stamina – Love being busy and productive. Always feel there is more to do and start each day ready to check off their list.

Activator – Make things happen by turning thoughts into action. They want to get busy accomplishing things now instead of merely discussing things.

Adaptability – Prefer to go with the flow. Takes life as it comes and prefers to discover the future one day at a time.

Analytical – Searches for reasons and causes in a given situation. They have an ability to consider a wide diversity of causes which may be in play.

Arranger – Strong organizer who can stay flexible as they go. They are good at considering how all the pieces fit best for maximum productivity.

Belief – Committed to certain foundational convictions that won't change in circumstances. They have a strong purpose in life, which is clearly defined by their core values.

Command – A strong presence in whatever situation they are in. They take control and find decision-making easy in the moment.

Communication – Easily put their thoughts into words in a variety of mediums. They make strong conversationalists and group presenters.

Competition – Tend to measure their progress against that of others around them. Love contests and strive to come out on top.

Connectedness – Trust in how things fit together and believe that all events have meaning and that very few things are coincidental.

Consistency – Committed to treating people in all relationships the same. They prefer and embrace rules, routines, policies and procedures, which everyone can understand and follow.

Context – Focused more on the past and interpret an understanding of the present by researching what led up to this moment or event.

Deliberative – Take serious care in making and reaching decisions. In their choices they anticipate that there will be obstacles to consider and prepare for.

Developer – Recognizes the potential in others and cultivates that reality. They see the small improvements and find satisfaction when signs of progress are clear.

Discipline – Enjoys routine, structure and all that goes with maintaining it. They love to create order in their environment and maintain it.

Empathy – Have an uncanny knack to sense feelings of others and can put themselves into the role or situation of the other individual.

Focus – Can take a direction, follow through, make corrections and keep the course until completion. They tend to sort out priorities and then act.

Futuristic – Often inspired by a future focus. Love to imagine what could be. They pour their energy into energizing others with what is still ahead.

Harmony – Consensus builder who tries to avoid conflict. A peacemaker who goes out of the way to find areas of agreement.

Ideation – Fascinated by ideas with an ability to pull together diverse things and find connections between realities that others might miss.

Includer – Very accepting of others. Are aware of individuals who may feel left out and will work to welcome them and draw them into the activity, group or event.

Individualization – Finds the differences in people intriguing and is good at building teams by showing people how they can work together and become productive.

Input – Tends to collect, organize and archive everything whether it is something tangible like data and information, or intangible like ideas. They will do this also with relationships and things.

Intellection – Their busy minds are introspective but they appreciate debates and discussions which require broader and diverse knowledge.

Learner – Always wanting to know more. Desiring to improve through knowledge. It is the process of learning rather than the completion of learning, which provides joy for them.

Maximizer – Aware of the strengths that others bring to elevate the achievement of the group. They are always looking to raise the good into the great, the strong into the superb.

Positivity – The contagious enthusiasm of these individuals shows they are upbeat and usually excited about whatever they are involved in.

Relator – Value and nurture close relationships. They enjoy satisfaction by working with friends to accomplish a task, a goal, a dream or something they have in common.

Responsibility – Have a strong commitment to do what they say they will do. Honesty and loyalty are values, which they embrace and practice.

Restorative – Solid ability to deal with difficulties and problems. They can figure out what is wrong and resolve it.

Self-Assurance – Confident in their ability to face risks, manage challenges, and maintain balance in their lives. A strong certainty that their decisions are appropriate for the situation or relationship.

Significance – Strive for a major impact through their independence. They choose projects or tasks based on how much it will impact the organization or relationships of those around.

Strategic – Clear at finding creative alternatives in finding a way forward. They have an uncanny ability to see the patterns and issues in any situation and understand how to move ahead.

Woo – Love the opportunity of meeting new people and drawing them into a relationship or situation. They love to build bridges and make connections with others.

There you go – quite the list. Maybe you see something you hadn't noticed before. Enjoy and celebrate the strengths already in place. Diversity is a beautiful thing.

6

Choosing the 12 Tasks

When my wife and I (Shel) wanted to set up a rite of passage for our four children, we had a general understanding of each of their strengths and weaknesses, just by living with them and observing them. Choosing which tasks are best for our children can come from what we find in a more formal assessment, as presented in the last chapter, as well as what we have already learned about our children while raising them. As we sat down to plan, we used Luke 2:40 as our guideline. "Jesus grew in stature and in wisdom in the eyes of man and of God." We wanted them to grow in their physical skills (stature), their mental skills (wisdom), their cultural and social skills (in their relationship to the people around them -mankind) and their spiritual life (in their relationship to God). We also wanted them to succeed and to enjoy their tasks, even if they were challenging. So we deliberately chose some of the tasks in areas where we knew they had strengths and could succeed and build on their already burgeoning ability. But we wanted them to be challenged to grow in areas of weakness as well. So we tried to find tasks that would be doable, even if difficult for them.

On a paper, we wrote down the four categories of tasks. Physical, mental, cultural/social and spiritual. Under the physical skills, we chose a task of running 30 miles in 30 days. We gave this same task to all four of our children. It seemed a reasonable requirement that would build some physical discipline (setting aside 15 minutes or so each day for this exercise) as well as laying a foundation of physical fitness as they moved into junior high and began trying out for sports teams. For our oldest son, Heath, this was an area of weakness. He did not like to exercise. After setting this task, it was very difficult, even running alongside him, to get him to run one mile. But now in his 40s, Heath remembers that he learned more from this task than from any other. "It actually hurt to push myself to do this task, but I learned the importance of doing hard things for a greater purpose."

For our third son Blake, this task was an area of strength. He loved getting out and playing sports and running. He'd get up in the morning and tell me he was going to run three miles instead of one, so he could have a few days off from waking up early. Then, without me running alongside to urge him along, he'd go out and run by himself. Both Heath and Blake went on to play high school sports and see that task as a key step in becoming athletes.

For our daughter Malindi, running 30 miles in 30 days seemed like a daunting task, but she accepted it. We happened to be living in Tacoma, Washington on a home assignment from our work in Kenya during part of her 12th year. We did the running task by going to Waughap Lake nearby. One lap around the lake was one mile. She didn't like running in the cold American weather. Her lungs hurt. Her legs hurt. I ran alongside, encouraging her to keep running, but my urging was not always well received. Then one day, I got help from an unexpected source. The cross-country coach from a nearby community college had his runners at the Lake for a run. He saw Malindi running and came over and asked how old she was. He said he liked her running form and that if she ever went to the community college, she should look him up. He wanted her on his cross-country team. That outside word of encouragement helped her to keep at her task until she completed it.

The first task in Heath's book was to camp out in a tent by himself and cook his own supper. I'm not sure if he was worried about this task, but we were as his parents! It came time to set up his tent and sleep by himself after charring a hotdog over a fire he'd made on his own. But there had been a number of home invasions near our mission station and a herd of buffalo had also moved into the forest nearby because of an ongoing drought. Would Heath be safe from attackers? Would a buffalo trample his tent? We thought of canceling the task. But we felt it was an important start to the 12 Tasks, so in the end we compromised and found Heath a place to set up his tent that was marginally in the forest, but close enough for him to shout out if he needed rescuing. He spent his night safely in his tent. And the solo campout became a feature task for all our children.

For each child we chose three or four tasks focusing on physical strength. For Reid, going to a soccer camp to improve his ball skills. For all three boys, Heath, Reid and Blake, to play a round of golf with their Dad. For all four of our children, the big physical task was to climb Mt Kenya up to Point Lenana at 16,000 feet above sea level. This climbing task required planning, practice and determination. All four of our kids succeeded in climbing to Point Lenana. We weren't trying to set the pace for any of them to become mountain climbers. But we saw value in the accomplishment of a days-long task that made them endure, step-by-step, up to the ice and snow where Mt Kenya straddled the equator. They all remember that climb. But some not so fondly.

My daughter Malindi, now 32, remembers receiving her 12 tasks. She wasn't surprised to see that one task required her to climb Mt Kenya. Her brothers had all done it. She says, "I was very afraid to do it. I still remember seeing a tree hyrax in the forest on the way up from the Met Station on the Naro Moru route. I did not feel good during the climb. I had a hard time getting to the top. I still remember having to use the outhouse at Austrian. It had no real door and it hung over a cliff with cold air coming up through the hole. I remember eating some freeze-dried meals. They didn't taste very good. But it was a bonding time with my Dad. Near the peak my Dad had to push from behind while the guide held me hand and dragged me along. I suffered windburn on my cheeks and also on my wrist, where the guide had pulled my glove away from the sleeve of my coat. At the top an Italian couple gave me a rehydrating drink. They were very worried about me, even though I was just having an emotional time. I felt miserable at the top of Pt Lenana, even though I'd made it. It felt better coming down. We came down quickly and had a celebration night at Naro Moru River Lodge. I never looked back on it as a memory of something I'd accomplished. I just thought of it as a miserable time."

As her father, I had used that trip to encourage her to persevere with her homework in high school, reminding her that if she had conquered Mt Kenya, she could conquer the mountain of homework. But for Malindi, apparently she felt she hadn't completed the task well. She and her husband were with us in Kenya in late 2020. Malindi says, "I decided to climb the mountain again at age 31, this time with my husband. We joined my brother Reid, who organized the climb for his 12-year-old son Max as one of Max's 12 Tasks. I wanted to have a better experience and to achieve the climb on my own terms as an adult. I felt I'd not done it well as a 12-year-old. This time, it felt amazing at the peak watching the sun spread over the landscape below. I had accomplished the climb without complaining or being dragged up by Dad and the guide."

A week shy of my 65th birthday, I made that climb up Mt Kenya with Malindi for a second time, as well as watching my son Reid help his son Max complete this task. It was a privilege to see Malindi's endurance on this hike, as well as to see my grandson Max blossom and push his way to the top. I had to hobble a bit on the way down with old aching knees, but I realized again the importance of pushing oneself to do hard things – for Max as a 12-year-old, for Malindi who was determined to do a better job and for an old man like me. As I forged my way up and later limped down the mountain, I was reminded of the lines from Rudyard Kipling's poem If. I was able to "force my heart and nerve and sinew to serve their turn long after they were gone, and so hold on when there was nothing in me except the will that says to them hold on."

My son Reid added fishing and birdwatching as physical tasks for his son Ian. Ian had always been fascinated by fishing, so Reid and his wife Sandy chose a fishing task as a way of adding to an existing strength. The fishing involved a 16-hour ride in a Land Rover to fish for Nile Perch in Lake Turkana, inviting me along as Ian's grandfather. Birdwatching was not a strength for Ian, but his parents wanted Ian to have a better appreciation of the natural world. Ian had to observe and identify 50 different bird species. To meet the deadline on this one, their family spent a day in Nairobi National Park. By the end of the day, the other family members had had their fill of bird watching, but Ian had his check list completed.

My son Blake picked up on this bird list task, but sent his daughter Maddie out with me, her grandfather, to find 50 species in a day. We managed it by driving between the Malewa River, where we live, to Lake Naivasha and Lake Elmenteita. Now Maddie's brother Quinn is working on his 12 tasks and his list includes finding 50 bird species in a day with Babu (grandpa).

One of the main tasks we set for our children for improving their mental skills was giving them a reading list. This allowed us to give them books appropriate to their personalities and interests. We also put several books about African topics like *Facing Mt Kenya* by Jomo Kenyatta and *Things Fall Apart* by Chinua Achebe and *Cry the Beloved Country* by Alan Paton and the *Maneaters of Tsavo* by John Patterson.

For social and cultural skills, we tried to push our children to learn more about the African culture where they lived. Heath's Ninth Task read: "Thou shalt go and live with Mama and Baba Mwaura for five days. You must not speak English and you must help in the shamba (farm)." In the end we cut the stay down to three days, and I'm sure Heath did speak to his hosts in English. But he learned how a typical Kenyan family lived in the rural area near Nakuru. Years later Heath said that staying at Solai in an African home was one of his most significant tasks. "I learned how others live, I spent a day being a matatu tout (collecting fare for a rural taxi), I milked a cow and I sprayed tomatoes using a backpack sprayer."

For spiritual growth, we gave each of our children some

kind of Bible study as well as Bible memory work. Heath did a study on the names of God. Malindi did a Bible study about God's covenant promises that my wife had written in story form – *Covenant on Matthews Mountain*.

Some tasks can be crafted to combine several of these areas together. One task that involved both physical and mental skills was having our children purchase the food and prepare a meal for others. Malindi cooked her meal for parents and grandparents. Reid and Blake created restaurants and invited friends to be their guests. As part of the task, they had to think through a menu, purchase the needed ingredients, make the food and even serve the meal. Blake added to his task by hiring some friends to be waiters for his Burko's Restaurant (paying them in leftover food!).

Our son Reid, who with his wife Sandy has created 12 tasks for each of his four children, combined spiritual growth with social skills by having their twins volunteer to teach Sunday School at our international fellowship in Naivasha. Ian mentioned that task recently as having been the most helpful in his spiritual growth. When I asked Reid how he chose tasks appropriate for their children, he said they had a core of three tasks that every one of their children had to do. First on the list was the solo campout that had featured in the lists of all four of our children. Apparently, that task really helped each of our children feel like they had grown up and conquered any fears of being alone in the dark in the middle of Africa. The other two were climbing Mt Kenya and the special meal near the end where they had "the talk" with their children.

Our son Blake, who is also doing 12 tasks for his children, combined physical and social and even spiritual tasks when his daughter Maddie learned to sew some cloth facemasks, which she then distributed to Kenyan Christian families in a nearby church during the beginning of the Covid era.

So as parents, it's up to you to choose tasks that are appropriate to your child, that take into account their talents and strengths as well as their weaknesses.

Another thing to remember when choosing tasks is to consider how much parental or adult involvement each task will take. Many tasks can push the child to take control and do the task on their own, like reading certain books or memorizing scripture. But others require parental time. This is a good thing. As my daughter said, even though she didn't enjoy her first climb up Mt Kenya, it was a bonding time with me. And for each of our children to climb the mountain I had to commit three or four days for the climb, in addition to the planning and purchasing of supplies. When our son Reid decided a long bike ride would be a good task for Max, it required Reid to ride with him. The 36 kilometer ride up the side of Eburru mountain to a geothermal spa required a full day of riding. They spent the night in rustic houses at the spa and eased sore muscles in the geothermal steam bath. Then they had to ride back the next day – over 80 kilometers of bike riding on rough roads with punctures.

Reid committed the time needed to help his first son Griffen complete his 12 Tasks. Reid managed one memorable task by taking Griffen out of school for a few days to accompany him on a work trip to Zanzibar, and then they tagged on a few days at the end of the trip to accomplish a unique task that took into account Griffen's youthful fascination of the ocean: swimming with whale sharks off Mafia Island. But the next year, when Reid and Sandy's twins, Ian and Lily, did their 12 tasks, it stretched the parents to the limit. They had to encourage the twins through a total of 24 tasks in one year. Reid and Sandy consolidated one task as they both climbed Mt Kenya with the twins. But it was an exhausting year. Reid commented, "The most important thing we found in giving our children 12 Tasks was it taught them they could push through and complete everything in a year." He didn't feel the tasks themselves were as important as the lesson of taking on the challenges and seeing them through to completion.

So, select tasks that will push your children to grow physically, mentally, socially and spiritually, and be sure to consider how much time you have to invest in helping your child complete their tasks.

Jack has his own take on choosing tasks for our children. Here's what Jack has to say:

For some of you, a hammer and saw are a comfortable part of who you are and what you do. I had a strong disability with tools. Pens and books are my world.

Choosing tasks for my son, which would show up my own inadequacies, is not something for the faint of heart. Yet vulnerability is essential in building that bond of trust between father and son or between mother and daughter or vice versa. A child must see that their parent is not afraid to try new things that they aren't good at.

Being a father means that you are doing more than just recreating another copy of yourself. A son or daughter should be given the chance to explore and experience a wide diversity of options available to young adults. And so we offered Richard the task of building a tree fort with just a hammer, a saw, some nails and whatever wood we could find. Remember the secret of the tasks is the character and confidence that is being built during the process.

The location for our tree fort was a seasoned wild olive tree in our back yard. Fifteen feet off the ground, the branches were splayed conveniently to set down a floor. Bracing and securing that floor required the agility of monkeys and the daring of a tiger. By setting up a ten foot ladder and a few wooden foot braces on a tree branch, we launched off on yet one more task.

Parents always seem to be busy with something. Setting apart time to help your son become a man often gets forgotten in the urgent requests of others. Not too many boys or girls are begging parents to set up 12 Tasks that will stretch them and challenge them. Friends may be calling, entertainment and community events and school may be scheduling up time. It is easy to just let time slip by as the inconvenience of the tasks start to surface.

But here is where the character begins to develop. As

the parent commits to a journey with their child, there is an adjustment in attitude and action that emerges like a Monarch butterfly from a chrysalis. An adjustment, not just in the child but in the parent.

You begin to see your child through new eyes. You begin to assess the unique design that God wove together in the tapestry of strengths, skills, passions, challenges and dreams that make up your son or daughter. It takes time, thought and tenderness but it is an investment which will yield returns far above any financial schemes calling for your heart.

You and your son or daughter are unique and their 12 Tasks should reflect it. When deciding on 12 Tasks, the key is finding a good balance of tasks that will encourage strengths, stimulate growth, help them learn new things and build relationships.

Encourage Strengths

Using your assessment as a starting point, sit down with your son or daughter, and make a list of their strengths. Come up with four possible tasks that will build on their strengths. For example, if they have potential as a writer, then you could give them a task to write a short story or conduct a study among their peers about what it is like to be a teenager. If they are gifted at sports, maybe they could organize a mini-tournament among their friends, with proceeds going to a good cause.

Learn New Things

What are some things your son or daughter has always wanted to do but has not taken the time to learn? Perhaps it is playing the guitar, juggling a soccer ball 100 times, or learning words in a new language. Maybe they have always wanted to ride a horse or start their own business. Incorporate some of these things into the 12 Tasks.

Build Relationship

It is hard to overstate the role a child's relationship with a parent (or another adult figure) has in their transition to being an adult – especially sons with fathers and daughters with mothers. Planning some tasks together—and in community—will provide you with lifelong memories and experiences that serve as bonding agents. Choose two to three tasks that you must accomplish together, even if they also stretch you as a parent. These will ideally be adventure-oriented and take you out of your normal world and routine.

Stimulate Growth

There will clearly be areas that are important to your youth's development where they have fears, feel intimidated or lack natural talent. But facing fears and overcoming challenges are instrumental for his or her development as an adult. Come up with four possible tasks that stretch your son or daughter and address their weaknesses. Don't push them too hard, though. Try to find the right balance and make sure they have some input.

We encourage you to identify a couple of tasks from your list (perhaps under Stimulate Growth or Learn New Things) that you do together with your 12 Tasks Community. This could be something like a five-day hike and canoe trip, a night on the streets of your city, or even a missions trip.

Here is what our son Richard's list looked like:

Encourage Strengths	Build Relationship
1. Write a 50-page book—include photos taken by you. 2. Give a two-minute talk at youth group. 3. Memorize the Sermon on the Mount. 4. Create your own radio-music tape with you as DJ.	1. Write 24 letters to different friends who live outside Kijabe. 2. Stay at a Kenyan national's home learning all you can about their family, life and culture. 3. Make a complete dinner for three friends (order, buy, cook and clean-up). 4. Survey other teens and write an article on "The Hardest Thing about Growing Up."

Learn New Things	Stimulate Growth
1. Build a Tree Fort in the back yard. 2. Learn 100 Swahili words. 3. (Took a stand against prejudice). 4. Juggle a soccer ball 50 times without stopping.	1. Read through the Bible in one year. 2. Climb Mt. Kenya—pack and organize your own gear (12 Tasks Community). 3. Run 120 miles outside class or sports. 4. Write about how God uniquely made you and list ten different career possibilities.

Making the final list: Choose which tasks are fundamental to your list and then let your son or daughter pick from among the remaining tasks to reach your 12. Try not to get too caught up in what others in your 12 Tasks Community are doing (other than as a source of ideas and inspiration). The point is not to have a carbon copy list but to craft something unique to your son or daughter.

You can use the following chart to organize your tasks, like the ones we offered to Richard.

Encourage Strengths	Build Relationship
1 2 3 4	1 2 3 4
Learn New Things	**Stimulate Growth**
1 2 3 4	1 2 3 4

Or you can use this chart to set up your tasks according to the
four categories that Shel and Kym used:

Physical	Social / Cultural
1.	1.
2.	2.
3.	3.
4.	4.
Mental	**Spiritual**
1.	1.
2.	2.
3.	3.
4	4.

7

Finding a Mentor

It can be helpful to involve another parent or adult you deeply admire in your journey. A man for your son or a woman for your daughter. They could be a Pastor or youth leader at your church or a neighbor who has a great relationship with his own son or daughter. You could also approach a coach or teacher with strong Christian values. Maybe you have a strong connection with your own parent or other relative and want to get their insight and perspective.

This step is not essential but it would certainly benefit to have someone more experienced engaged in the 12 Tasks journey from the beginning. This is a person you can ask questions of, who can help assess your relationship with your son or daughter and who can support you with your young teen about doing 12 Tasks together. This is someone who you believe models what it means to be an adult and who can help you recognize what is truly important. This is someone who truly cares about you but is not afraid to ask the tough questions.

In their monumental work *Spiritual Leadership*, Henry and Richard Blackaby state that: "Tragically, many people who are great leaders in public for whatever reason leave their problem-solving ability, people skills, and team-building instincts at the front door when they return home to their families. While this is not a book about parenting, it should be stated that there is no greater leadership position you can hold than being a parent. Whether you see yourself as a leader or not, if you are a parent, you owe it to your children to learn to lead as effectively as possible."[15](p. 17)

15   Blackaby, Henry and Richard, Spiritual Leadership (B&H Publishing: Nashville, Tennessee), p. 17

Building a Community - A Word Especially to Fathers

One of the biggest mistakes we make as men is isolating ourselves from other men. We easily equate true manhood with the rugged individual and the maverick. It is very helpful to undertake 12 Tasks with other dads and their sons. This is the support community that will help you keep going when it gets tough. And you may be surprised about friendships you build that will last long after 12 Tasks is complete.

Wes Yoder, in his book, *Bond of Brothers*, says, "Too often, our fathers walk through our lives as silent heroes or mysterious, distant figures. Male, but undefined; man, but opaque in silence. How often have you heard or said, 'my dad doesn't say very much' or, 'I didn't know my father all that well?' This is a cry that grows from a wince in the heart of a young boy to something much worse in the chest of a grown man, finding himself falling into the pattern of 'like father, like son,' wishing he could call that man 'friend'"[16]

Moms and their girls may find it easier to gravitate toward building a shared community with other mothers and daughters but in this age of business that is no longer something which can be taken for granted. Shared oversight of the developing adulthood is something to strive for so they are enriched from adults with diverse strengths.

But how do you build that community? Maybe you are fortunate and you are reading this book because another parent has already approached you about doing 12 Tasks. But if not, you will actually want to think carefully about approaching two or three other parents who have sons or daughters the same age. Start with those whose sons or daughters are already friends with your child. It will go a long way towards convincing your son or daughter to participate.

Try to meet together a few times before launching out on your 12 Tasks journey to compare notes and discuss how you will overcome inevitable challenges you face along the way.

16   Wes Yoder, Bond of Brothers – Connecting with Other Men Beyond Work, Weather and Sports (Zondervan: Grand Rapids, MI, 2013) p. 17.

Yoder, once again, says, "When fathers are missing or silent, it is more difficult for a boy or young man to discover his manhood. It is not easy for a young man to civilize or enlighten himself, and a healthy balance of game and story, rooted in the essence and presence of his father, is meant to help him on his way. The true narrative of a father creates a lifelong point of reference as a young man learns to create and tell his own story. This is so because a father's narrative includes for his sons, and in perhaps even more powerful ways for his daughters, a living portrait of his character, his work ethic, his life, his ability to create, his desire to serve, and his capacity to play. As a father, you are the nearest point of reference your children will ever have to what the words Dad, man, husband, and father actually mean during their formative years and throughout their entire lives."[17]

For those without present fathers, mentors form an important link into maturity and understanding.

Shel says one easy place to find a mentor is within your own family – perhaps a grandparent or another relative who has a significant relationship with the child. I (Shel) was pleased when one of my grandson Ian's tasks said he was to join his dad (Reid) and grandfather (me) on an epic trip to Lake Turkana to catch a Nile Perch. When Ian's school had a long weekend, Reid and I packed his Land Rover and we drove almost 14 hours to Loyengelani and camped at an oasis on the southeast corner of Lake Turkana. The next day Reid bargained with local fisherman and we hired a wooden boat and loaded the fishing gear into the boat. We had some very high waves at times and we fished most of the morning, without catching anything. But eventually in the early afternoon, at a good spot off South Island, I felt a hit on my big wooden lure. I immediately handed the rod to Ian, who steadily brought in a 14-pound Nile Perch. We didn't catch any more fish that day, but after a rough crossing back to Loyengelani, we had a wonderful meal of the fish. Ian had caught his Nile Perch. He'd accomplished

---

17   Yoder, p. 55.

his task. And as his grandfather, I'd had a chance to be with him and encourage him on the patience needed to be a fisherman.

A year later, my son Blake added my name to one of the tasks for his daughter, Maddie. "Join Babu (Swahili for grandfather) and find and identify 50 bird species in one day," the task read. Maddie and I had a special day, starting at 7 am tramping through the dew. We had over 20 bird species on our list before breakfast. Then we drove through some savannah habitat for different birds, and ended our day at Lake Elmenteita where Flamingoes, Pelicans and African Spoonbills helped us to reach 50 species just after lunch time.

As I write this, I just helped Maddie's brother Quinn, who is doing his 12 Tasks this year, to find 50 bird species in a day. I guess the first task with me as a mentor on birding had been a hit, and Quinn and I completed the task before noon and then drove to Java House in Naivasha for a milkshake.

Last week Quinn finished part one of three parts for a task, which involved preparing three different meals for four or more guests. We'd been invited to have General Tso's chicken and apple pie, which Quinn had prepared. The task had not been easy for Quinn and he and his Mom had experienced some stress in getting everything done for that meal. But as we debriefed with Blake and Nicole, Quinn's parents, they felt it might be good if my wife Kym, Quinn's Kokoo (Maasai for grandmother) might be a good mentor for his next meal prep. That will take place soon.

For our son Heath, one of his tasks was to use ropes and climb to the peak of Fischer's Tower, a craggy volcanic cone in the middle of Hell's Gate near Naivasha. I had no idea how to climb with ropes, but Colin Densham, a fellow missionary who had coached and mentored me when I learned to play rugby in high school, was an accomplished climber. We asked Colin if he could teach Heath the basics of rock climbing and scale Fischer's Tower together. Colin provided the equipment and we went to Hell's Gate. Colin went ahead of Heath, anchoring the rope at various points. I stood at the bottom, belaying the rope.

My other two sons, Reid and Blake, watched. At one point, Heath couldn't reach the next finger hold. Colin was above him, encouraging him to reach just a little further. He told him not to fear, I had the rope belayed. In his reaching Heath did slip, but the rope held, and Colin calmly talked Heath across the rock until he had a firm grip and scrambled to the top.

After Heath made it to the top, Colin taught him how to abseil (also known as rappelling in North America), leaning back on his rope and walking down the rock face with his feet. Later in the day, Colin taught me and the other boys how to climb up a nearby chimney in a volcanic cliff. We all made it up and then abseiled down. When the day was over, Heath had another task done, with the help of a mentor, a man who had been significant in my growth as a teen. And we'd made it into a fun family day for the other boys in the family.

John and Melissa Eager, who work in Tanzania, have done 12 Tasks with their three children, felt free to call on another adult for help with one of their tasks. Melissa writes: "While for the most part, it's important for the same sex parent/adult to be guiding the tasks, both parents can and should get involved at different times for different tasks. If this isn't possible, ask someone else to help out. In our family, when it came to cooking a meal, it was mom who gave instruction. When it came to things like changing a tire, it was dad. One of our sons showed an interest in fishing, so one of his tasks was to catch fish. Neither of us knew much about fishing or even knew where to go. So we asked a good friend to help out and he took my husband and son fishing and chose a place where he knew they would actually catch fish. They returned earlier than expected and I was surprised and dismayed to discover that they brought back the catch but had not gutted and cleaned the fish! Time for mom to step in! If you are going to catch fish, you gotta clean 'em and eat 'em! So I helped my son gut and clean the fish since I had some minimal experience."

Call on the experts who have the knowledge you don't. In a world paralyzed by fear where overwhelmed and overfunctioning parents try to control their child's world to the point of bubble-wrapped protection, it is good to free your child to take risks that make a difference.

Or, as Elon Musk, with his self-driving Tesla smart cars, his colonies on Mars expeditions, his spaceships designed for civilian experience, and his other artificial intelligence projects, did when he became dissatisfied with his children's private school education, start your own thing. He believed that children should be taught to solve problems and not just be given tools. He believed that educators should start with the problem and work backward rather than handing over memorized equations. He believed that incentive improves when you are dealing with real people and real problems.

Having said this, realize that the future our teens are stepping into is far different than the one we transitioned into. Journalist Benjamin Stetcher describes it as "a world filled with artificial intelligence, genetic engineering, automation, virtual reality, personalized medicine, self-driving cars, and people on Mars. A world where people might not even have jobs and where society itself may be arranged in fundamentally different ways. How are parents, and society for that matter, supposed to know how to prepare them to succeed in a world that we cannot predict?"[18]

Tim Elmore, who has spoken to over 500,000 "educators, parents, coaches and employers" notes that today's parents are frustrated and fearful. Frustrated because the rapid changes around them are opening a generation gap wider than they can traverse. Culture, society and peers have constant access to the ones we are trying to influence. Fear comes from the news cycle with its stories of "terror, school shootings, drug abuse, cyber-bullying, abductions, and human trafficking."[19] The constant barrage is like a verbal tsunami that keeps us reactionary to the thousands of fears we can't control. Overprotecting our children only serves to make them more fragile than ever.

18   Tim Elmore and Andrew McPeak, Generation Z Unfiltered – Facing Nine Hidden Challenges of the Most Anxious Population (Poet Gardener: Atlanta, GA, 2019), p.4.
19   Elmore, p. 12

Grant Schofield, a professor in Auckland, New Zealand discovered some interesting realities from his intervention at a primary school where hyper-safety concerns had backlashed into increased bullying and diminished student engagement. He issues a warning to parents overly concerned with the challenges facing their child. "Too many rules can have an adverse effect on children. The great paradox of sheltering is that it's more dangerous in the long run. Society's obsession with protecting kids ignores the benefits of risk taking. Children develop the frontal lobe of their brain when taking risks, meaning they work through consequences. You can't teach them that. They have to learn risk on their own terms. It doesn't develop watching TV. They have to take a risk."[20]

During the first six years of a child's life, the parent will micro-manage with simple and clear instructions, using positive and negative reinforcement. During the second six years the parent becomes a manager, yielding increased autonomy and responsibility with appropriate increased freedoms. In the third six years, the ones we are focusing on with 12 Tasks, the parent will become more of a supervisor as the child develops abstract thinking. Here, the passing on of life skills is important and a parent will coach their child into making better decisions. During the fourth six-year block, the parent becomes a consultant, offering experiences through other mentors and working to solidify a strong relationship.[21]

We had an ideal village setting where parents with similar ideals and values were able to share the care of sons and daughters. You may not have that same physical reality but you may be able to reproduce it in a neighborhood, a church community, or in a city with like-minded parents. Elmore says, "I believe it truly does 'take a village' to raise good kids. Reject the competitive parenting model we see so often and create a community of parents in your neighborhood or town who will help keep watch over your kids' play time."[22]

20   Elmore, p. 72
21   Elmore, p. 73
22   Elmore, p. 76

Use the skills of potential mentors in your extended community to cross-pollinate the strength of all of those invested and involved in the 12 Tasks. Provide instruction, demonstrations, experiences and assessments that will provide confidence, clarity, direction and life skills. If you, as the parent, don't have the skills, expertise or even the time to oversee each task, look for men and women who can help mentor your child through one of their tasks.

PART 3

DOING THE 12 TASKS

Presenting the 12 Tasks

My wife Kym and I (Shel) chose our son Heath's 12th birthday as the occasion to present him with his 12 tasks. It seemed to us the most appropriate time. We usually had a special birthday party every year for each of our children. We could make this one just a bit more special and invite some of Heath's teachers and adult family members and friends, as well as Heath's friends from school.

One year after this presentation birthday, our son would be 13, and entering into the teen years is often seen as a big milestone. So we thought giving him his 12 tasks, and 12 months to complete them before he hit 13 would be a good fit.

There is nothing magical or sacred about giving the presentation at your child's 12th birthday. We know friends who have done it a year or two later. Or they have chosen a different occasion for presenting the tasks.

Whatever date or occasion you choose, it is important to make the presentation special, a time when your son or daughter is called to attention, called to adventure, called to a quest, called to complete 12 Tasks of adulthood.

In the book of Joshua chapter 4 God performed a miracle and held back the water from the flooding Jordan River so the people of Israel could cross over on dry land. Once they had crossed, Joshua ordered 12 men to pick up 12 stones from the river bed. These were big enough stones that they needed to be hefted on the shoulders of men. Joshua had them heap up the 12 stones in a big pile at their campsite that night. The stones were to stand as a memorial. Joshua said, "When your children ask you, 'What do these stones mean?' tell them that the flow of the Jordan was cut off before the ark of the covenant of the LORD. When it crossed the Jordan, the waters of the Jordan were cut off. These stones are to be a memorial to the people of Israel forever."

A memorial is something to help us remember. And that is the basic purpose of the celebration where we present our son or daughter with their 12 Tasks.

In order for a memorial to mean anything, it needs witnesses. The first and most obvious witnesses are people. So for your presentation be sure to invite people. The immediate family, for sure. The grandparents if they are available. Your child's friends. Teachers, coaches, Sunday school teachers and others who have played a role in your child's life. These people will witness the memorial and remember it.

Just a few months ago I got an email from Mutugi M'Narobi, a school friend of Heath's who was invited to his 12 Tasks birthday party. Mutugi began by saying he remembered this special party where we'd given Heath some tasks to complete. Mutugi went on to say that his firstborn daughter was approaching her 12th birthday and he wondered if I could give him any advice on how to set up a similar set of challenges for his daughter. The memory of that party had stuck with Mutugi and he remembered it. I shared with him some of the rough draft chapters from this book so Mutugi and his wife could give their daughter 12 tasks.

Having friends and family and mentors as witnesses to the memorial also creates a community of those who care who can encourage your son or daughter or ask how they're doing or what task they're working on.

The second witness should be written. After a victory over the Amalekites in Exodus 17, God tells Moses in verse 14: "Write this down as something to be remembered." Spoken words are good, but they can easily be forgotten. So when God wanted an event to be remembered, he told Moses to write it down.

We provided our written witness by presenting Heath with a book. The book opened with two letters, one from me and one from my wife. We told Heath why we were giving him the tasks and that we believed in him and that these challenges would help him as he moved into adulthood. When I visited my son Heath a year ago, he still had his 12 Tasks book and those letters were both still there, as a memorial.

My letter to Heath began: "February 26, 1991, Dear Heath, You are 12 years old today. As you approach your teen years and becoming a man, you will face many new and challenging situations…"

We're told that a picture is worth 1000 words, so we provided Heath with a pictorial witness. The book we gave him was one of those old photo albums with a see-through plastic page that you could pull up. There were thin ribs of tacky (not sticky) glue where you could place photos. Each task was written on paper, in a banner-type headline and stuck to the top of the page, leaving space below for photos showing the task being completed.

Heath's completed picture book has photos of him on top of Mt Kenya, standing beside Mr Njoroge in his Peugeot 404 pickup matatu (taxi) and more. There was even a photo of the presentation birthday with Mutugi sitting next to Heath!

And lastly, there should be a spoken witness to this event. I don't remember what I said, but after the birthday cake and ice cream and presents, we had everyone sit around the room with Heath on a chair near the middle. I then told everyone the purpose of Heath's 12 Tasks and prayed for him in the year ahead.

Then my wife gave him his book, and he paged through it and the witnesses saw and heard what tasks he had been given.

Not everyone gives their children all 12 Tasks at the same time. Lew and Brandy Johnson from Nairobi heard about 12 Tasks and decided to create their own rite of passage for their first born daughter. They also chose her 12th birthday for the presentation. But on that day, they only gave her the first task.

They explained that she had a month to complete that task, and at the beginning of the next month, she would receive the second task, and so on until her 13th birthday. So the Johnsons set up 12 separate presentations throughout the year. This kept each task fresh and helped their daughter finish each task on time and gave anticipation for the next one to be revealed.

The Johnsons felt this gave them the ability to adjust tasks as the year went on. If one task proved very difficult, they could shuffle the tasks and give one the next month that would be more enjoyable.

Each of our other three children also received their 12 Tasks challenge and book at their 12th birthday party. And in the past few years, we have attended the 12th birthday parties for many of our grandchildren and watched them receive their 12 Tasks.

As you prepare to give your child their 12 Tasks, choose a date a time and a place where your child can be celebrated. It might be their 12th birthday. It can be another date of your choosing. But be sure to make it a special event so your child will realize the importance of the 12 Tasks as well as your honoring him or her and setting them on their course to adulthood in a memorable way.

Creating a Timeline to Complete the 12 Tasks

In order to help your child complete their 12 Tasks, it's important to chart out a timeline over the next year. Key markers and times for assessing progress will be very important here. Start with the end in mind and plan the date for your celebration ceremony. Then work backwards and schedule dates for group tasks and tasks that need to be accomplished during a specific time period. The rest of the tasks can be accomplished at any time in the year but spacing them out evenly over three-month increments is strongly recommended. Here is a sample timeline, which can serve as example of how a 12 Tasks list can be scheduled.

Begin with the end date in mind. To make it easy to visualize, let us assume a birthday on January 21st. Realize that other responsibilities like school work, community involvement and church commitments need to be factored in to how much time a task will take. Consider also the time of year when certain tasks should be done. Outdoor adventure tasks may work best in summer or winter holidays. Tasks requiring memorization or creativity may work best in times of challenging weather. Having a clear start and finish date allows for planning but also can create a buffer in the next section if your son or daughter falls behind a little.

Some tasks will take a few hours or days and some will be spread out over months. Take this into consideration as you discuss and set out a timeline with your young teen.

Sample Timeline for 12 Tasks -

Start Date	Completion Date	Task to Accomplish	Details to Consider
12th Birthday	January 21st	Present the 12 Tasks with friends present	Prepare the book listing the 12 Tasks chosen – photos and significant mementos will be kept in here.
January 21	February 21	Tasks 1-2 Map out when each task is done	Choose one easy and one challenging task – record significant moments.
Feb 21	March 21	Task 3	A challenging task that requires some focus.
March 21	April 21	Task 4	An easier task requiring indoor activity.
April 21	May 21	Task 5	A challenging task – change it up between mental, physical or social tasks.
May 21	June 21	Task 6	A harder task that takes some focus and output to stimulate investment at the half-way mark.
June 21	August 21	Tasks 7,8,9	Single event tasks requiring extra energy and time commitment work well during holidays. These can work well as group events with others involved in the 12 Tasks.
August 21	September 21	Task 10	Provide some incentives and encouragement with a rewarding task.
September 21	October 21	Task 11	Create some space for challenging tasks which take more time.

October 21	November 21	Task 12	Support your child through this final task and allow some space to finish up before the celebration.
November 21	January 21	Buffer	Prepare for completion of tasks unfinished – fill in the gaps – polish up the book and celebration event features.
	13th Birthday	Celebration Event	Contact significant mentors, friends and relatives – Plan a celebration weekend as an award for completion.

Some projects are going to take careful thought and planning and some will be done quickly. Because I (Jack) worked in Kenya far from the shopping center in Nairobi, when my daughters had to do something involving hospitality then we had to wait until Gayle's bi-monthly shopping trip to get supplies. Otherwise we had to make do with what could be found locally. When the girls needed to make shorts, they had to plan for a term break to head into town to choose material, thread and patterns. The timeline for your 12 Tasks should consider where you live in regard to how accessible supplies are plus time and resources needed to assemble them.

Let's say you have a little more complicated task like a climb up a mountain distant from your residence. My son, Richard, had such a task for his son Jordan but Covid hit and that one seemed out of reach since the mountain was in another country out of bounds when travel restrictions fell into place.

Richard, Michelle and Laura all had to climb Mt Kenya for their culmination task. For my sake, Michelle and Laura did their trip together so that was considered in planning their task timeline. Michelle's climb was her last task and the same climb was Laura's first task.

Here are a few steps you might want to follow for bigger tasks.

1. Clarify exactly what the task is going to be, who is going to be involved and when that task needs to be accomplished.
2. Create a structure breaking down the work needed. For example:
   a. Determine a date for the climb during a term break
   b. Recruit others to participate in the adventure
   c. Consider the budget necessary for the adventure and secure resources
   d. Book the guides, route dates, and lodge rooms
   e. Exercise at altitude with climbs, running, lifting, etc.
   f. Purchase necessary supplies and equipment for the hike
   g. Meet to plan, prepare and pray
3. Break each section into specifics
   a. Date for climb?
      • Research when the weather is best for climbing
      • Research which route would be best for teens
      • Research which dates are still available (with limited cabins and guides)
      • Research which companies are available and at which times
      • Research when others who might want to go are available
   b. Recruit others to participate in the adventure
      • Contact friends or classmates who might be interested in the climb
      • Contact parents to see who is willing to invest in this adventure
      • Ask local parents if they have contacts who might wish to go
      • Consider contacts and friends who aren't local to tap interests
   c. Consider the budget necessary for the adventure and secure resources
      • Research costs for the adventure

- Consider resources available in house
- Determine how the balance will be raised in the time allotted
    - Donations
    - Fees from others participating
    - Fundraising projects
    - Crowd Funding

4. Determine the project dependencies

a. Determine what must be done in order before another step can be taken

- Everyone must be consulted and agree to the dates before booking
- Resources need to be in place before confirming the lodge, guide, etc.
- Personal fitness needs to be confirmed over the six months prior
- Adequate equipment and clothing needs to be purchased in advance
- Familiarity with video and photo equipment needs to be gained
- All legal, safety and country guidelines need to be understood in advance

Some of you might like a flow chart as you prepare. Others, familiar with the task and terrain, will be able to almost fly by the seat of your pants.

Sample Flow Chart:

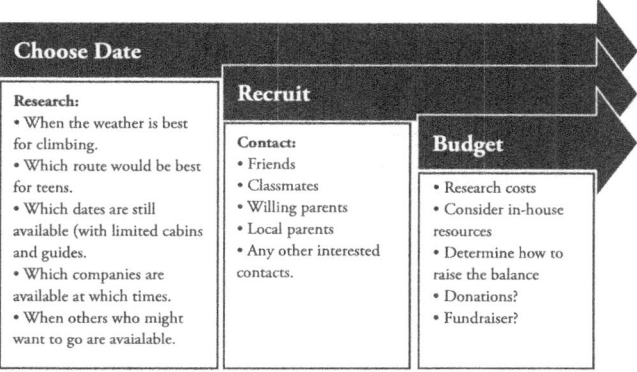

Choose Date

Research:
- When the weather is best for climbing.
- Which route would be best for teens.
- Which dates are still available (with limited cabins and guides.
- Which companies are available at which times.
- When others who might want to go are avaialable.

Recruit

Contact:
- Friends
- Classmates
- Willing parents
- Local parents
- Any other interested contacts.

Budget
- Research costs
- Consider in-house resources
- Determine how to raise the balance
- Donations?
- Fundraiser?

5. Determine Time Needed

Review the dependency chart and allocate the time needed for each step along the way. You can see why limiting the number of monumental tasks is necessary if you plan to finish within the year's time limit. Of course, the 12 Tasks leave you in control of setting up what will be done and when it will be done.

Using our plan above we add in time needed:

Create a structure breaking down the work needed. For example:

    a. Determine a date for the climb during a term break
        January 6-10 hrs

    b. Recruit others to participate in the adventure
        February 4-6 hrs

    c. Consider the budget necessary for the adventure and secure resources 2-4 hrs

    d. Book the guides, route dates, and lodge rooms
        March 2-4 hrs

    e. Exercise at altitude with climbs, running, lifting, etc.
        Jan-July 5 hrs a week

    f. Purchase necessary supplies and equipment for the hike
        May-June 3-4 hrs

g. Meet to plan, prepare and pray
   Jan-July weekly 1 hr.

7. Search for shareable resources to cut costs etc.

Quite likely there are others in your social circle who have access to some of the equipment you need. They may be willing to share it, loan it or make it available at a cheaper price.

8. Highlight Key Milestones along the way to everyone involved. Email, WhatsApp, Facebook, Instagram – all makes this easy.

   a. We have our date set!
   b. We now have ten of us committed!
   c. We're in May and we already have half our budget met!
   d. We're scheduling a rock climb in the valley next Saturday for practice!
   e. Last major shopping trip coming up. Let us know if you need anything.

9. Chart it out

You can make this simple or complex, depending on your personality and your love for detail. Different members of the team going on this adventure may have different gifts and things can be delegated so it isn't too heavy for any one participant. The value of meeting regularly with others is that it allows this to happen. If you keep it all to yourself and your own family bubble then you can make this work for you and your style. The important thing is to not make things so difficult that you want to give up before you get going.

When all is said and done. Just do it the best you can and when you can.

Completing the Tasks

DO IT!

Designing tasks together with your son or daughter is a challenge. But actually accomplishing those tasks in the midst of busy schedules and multiple pressures will require dedication and accountability.

Having a mentor, a 12 Tasks Community, and a defined schedule with check-in times for accountability and adjustment will help you.

You will also want to make sure you take lots of pictures and journal the experience along the way. Richard, Michelle and Laura still have the special book their parents (Jack and Gayle) put together to mark the 12 Tasks journey.

Here are some other tips to help you on the journey

Be strategic about your involvement in supporting your son or daughter. Think about the tasks where they will most need your involvement and encouragement and be intentional about providing it. But also be clear with them about tasks where they can ask for your input but must accomplish on their own.

Be organized without being too prescriptive. Keeping your son or daughter to basic goals and timelines through regular check-ins will be very important but be flexible about how your son or daughter actually accomplishes their tasks. They may do it differently from you. That's okay!

Make room in your schedules for the 12 Tasks. Today's sons and daughters have hardly had time, in many cases, to enjoy childhood because parents have enrolled them in so many learning programs, teams and groups so they don't fall behind their peers. On the other hand, outgrowing childishness is being delayed with driver's licenses, jobs and moving out happening later. We are working for age-appropriate autonomy and responsibility through well designed tasks.

Don't get into the comparison game: Your son or daughter is unique and it will be easy for you to compare them to their friends, something they will be doing anyway. Avoid trying to motivate them with phrases like, "I can't believe you have not finished this yet! Jackson finished three months ago." Or "Why is building this birdhouse so hard for you?" Or "Peter and his Dad renovated an entire basement suite together!" When you do need to challenge your son or daughter do it against the commitments they have made and not where others are at in their own journey.

Help the rest of the family to become cheerleaders: Family members who are impacted but peripheral to the 12 Tasks can still have a critical role, especially in cheering your son or daughter on towards the finish line. There are key moments where they will need the support of both parents or a sibling. Get them excited about what this means for the entire family and encourage them to cheer your son/daughter on along the way.

Remain flexible. The unexpected will happen! So, prepare yourself. Remain flexible enough to adjust plans when necessary. Perhaps a task proves harder than you thought and needs to be modified. Maybe the one-year time frame proves too short and needs to be extended, for a whole variety of reasons. The purpose of 12 Tasks is not to box you in but to give you a path to follow.

Be on the lookout for the extraordinary: Catch your son or daughter doing right, something unexpected but extraordinary. There are times where you will see them exhibiting values and qualities you are looking to instill outside of the scope of the 12 Tasks. Reward them for it. They will never forget it. In Richard's case, he received credit for an initiative he took (taking a stand against prejudice) that clearly demonstrated his growth and maturity and was able to substitute this for another task. Jack wrote and signed a certificate identifying what he had seen in Richard.

Pray together regularly. 12 Tasks can be done even if you do not have a faith background, but having one certainly helps. We are committed Christians and believe in an all-powerful but personal God, who takes a keen interest in our lives, and answers prayer. It makes a big difference to bring your joys and challenges during the 12 Tasks journey to the one who made your son or daughter in the first place.

You will not do this perfectly. At times it will be messy. That's real life and part of becoming a young adult is learning who we are and establishing a solid foundation for this greater life journey and for eternity. But it can be done. And you will find so much to celebrate.

One of the most special aspects of 12 Tasks is doing certain of the tasks together with your child. For Richard and I (Jack), one of those together-tasks was climbing Mt Kenya. As we climbed, I had to face my own fears, failures and shortcomings. I had to face up to several internal realities when taking my son up Mount Kenya for his final task.

One of the most agonizing moments with my son came when I realized that I couldn't reach the peak, the very thing I had asked him to do. On the day we reached Shipton's Camp for the last stop before summiting Mt Kenya, I found I had used up all my physical reserves. We were just 700 vertical meters short of our goal at Point Lenana. A four-hour scramble up the scree before sunrise would finish this task, but it might as well have been a million marathons for me on this day.

Altitude sickness can be fatal and has claimed a number of lives on Mt Kenya. So we had climbed slowly to allow our bodies to acclimatize. We had successfully made it up through stunning U-shaped glacial valleys. We had started our hike through dense bamboo forest with signs of elephant, then continued through the rich montane forest. Above the tree line, we passed the strange looking Giant Lobelias and Senecio plants. The towering peaks of Batian, Nelion and Lenana provided breathtaking images once we broke through cloud cover. Our guides had urged us forward with their steady chant of, "Take another step, it's just there."

I felt that my reputation was at stake and climbing a mountain when you've recently had the flu may not have been the wisest choice. But this day had been set, the money had been paid, and I wanted to give it my best shot. I felt like my fatherhood was on the line. Other fathers before me had done this and other fathers on this trip were ready to go.

The night's rest at Shipton's Camp didn't settle my heaving stomach. Not having been able to take in any nourishment for the first two days didn't help either. When the call came to wake up for our hike to the summit at about 2 am, I couldn't even lift my head off the pillow. Sometimes, willpower can only take you so far. The group delayed as long as they could, but I was going nowhere.

Depending on others became critical. The other men assured me they could take care of my son. Brian, Mark and Matt were all trustworthy friends. And yet, this is the vulnerability of manhood; admitting that sometimes others can take your son (or daughter) to places you aren't able to go yourself. And they did. They piled extra blankets on me and forged out into the darkness.

I felt an agonizing sense of failure wash over me despite the many good reasons I had for falling short of my dreams. All I was left with were dry heaves and a body frozen to the core.

Although I would later summit on another trip at another time with my daughters to prove I could climb to the top, the only thing I wished for on that dark morning was for the strength to summit with my son.

Losing that experience meant losing the memories we had planned to share. Part of the purpose of doing these tasks was to create bonding and memories of things shared together. When I failed to emerge for that final climb with my son, we would forever have a gap in our shared experiences and memories. At least that's the way I felt when I wasn't heaving.

My son went up in the darkness as a boy and came down in the light as a man. Mt Kenya, this volcanic giant, which geologists believe had once been the highest ice capped peak in Africa, had been conquered.

When the victorious men and their charges returned sometime later in the morning, the next test arose. The entire mountain had to be descended that very day and there was no way I was doing it on a stretcher. I gained strength from my son's accomplishment and we made the downward trek together. Sometimes the one who you had hoped to strengthen becomes the strength that you yourself need.

Once again, the rock hyrax scrambled for cover as we stumbled past. The cape buffalo watched defiantly on the lower slopes. The Kikuyu and Embu porters delivered us safely to our lodging. While they awarded me a certificate along with the rest, I knew that I'd missed the last climb to the summit with my son and my heart hurt at the loss.

One of the beauties of the tasks is that whether there is success or failure on the parent's part, there will be bonding and memories which neither child or parent can anticipate. When I see the pictures of my son raising his arms in celebration at the peak, and believing that he finished the task for both of us, it still brings tears to my eyes.

My wife claims I looked like death warmed over when I stumbled in, but my son was triumphant. While the picture of victory often would leave a pit in my stomach at my own failure to escort him all the way, it somehow makes his completed task more special. He did it without me then, just like he will have to do many more things without me in the future. And while he did it without me, he didn't do it alone. Somehow, I know, this makes a difference.

When you Fail to Complete a Task in Time

Richard recalls a time when he interviewed a government minister in a small African country that was trying to overcome a horrific past. They had bold goals for the future and many doubted these goals could be accomplished. "What do you say to people who look at this vision and say it cannot be done, that it is far too ambitious, that it is unrealistic?" Richard asked. The minister paused for a second and then responded: "Even if we reach 70% of our goals we will be much farther ahead than where we are now. It would be far better to try and fall short than not to try at all."

It is important to finish the tasks within the allotted time. This teaches our children the importance of sticking to a job and completing it. However, sometimes you will run into unavoidable circumstances. We're in the middle of sorting out how to live with the Covid-19 pandemic. My (Shel's) grandson Max started his tasks in the middle of school shut downs and international flight bans to Kenya, as well as limited travel between certain counties because of infection rates. One of his tasks was to spend a few nights in a Kenyan home to learn a bit about their culture. However, completing that task took on a lot more risk with the Covid scare. So Reid approached me and asked if I could set it up for Max to join me and one of my Kenyan pastors to show the Jesus film. I had just received new equipment for showing the film in our Dorobo villages. I had a plan to go to the home of Pastor Musanga Omerae in the Moidapi area. I would show him how to operate the equipment, we'd have a showing for the neighboring families (Kenya had laws against gatherings larger than 15 at the time). Then I'd leave the equipment with Pastor Musanga to show the film in surrounding villages. I invited Max to join me on this trip as an exchange for his village-living task. Max seemed excited to join me – maybe because he realized a three-day task had been reduced to one evening. We drove an hour-and-a-half to Pastor Musanga's house and met his family. We wore our masks and drank chai, sweet, milky Kenyan tea with a hint of woodsmoke.

As I tried to set up the various pieces of equipment, Max jumped in and helped me put things together. I had no idea where the solar charging matt was, but Max found a hidden compartment in the back to the big backpack and withdrew the solar panels, which could be used to charge the battery pack between showings. We set up the portable screen on a wall of the house and with an audience of about 16 young people we showed the Jesus film in the Maasai language. Max didn't understand any Maasai, but watched the film along with our Dorobo friends. At the end two of the teens who had watched the film prayed to receive Christ as their Savior. We prayed for them, left the equipment with Pastor Musanga and drove back under the moonlight, avoiding giraffe and zebra on the late night trip home.

It wasn't the task Max had been assigned in his 12 Task book, but extraordinary times had called for a change of plans.

My granddaughter Maddie, was also finishing her 12 Tasks in July 2020, when the Covid restrictions came into effect. She also had a village living task, but her parents decided there might be too much risk of getting infected with Covid. So Blake asked me to set up a one day hike through the Eburru Forest with some of our Dorobo hunters as guides. We had a great hike. The Dorobo men smoked the bees out of one of their beehives and we ate the golden forest honey. We hiked up a high ridge, before descending into a deep ravine. Our goal was to have lunch at a waterfall the Dorobo called Oreiyiet lolpul, the waterfall of the meat feast. They had given it that name in remembrance of a buffalo they had once killed and feasted on for a week beside the waterfall. At the bottom of the ravine, we encountered a massive landslide which had carried away our path and blocked us from reaching the waterfall. We had lunch there, found a gap in the trees to see part of the waterfall from a distance and headed home. Maddie had learned a lot about Dorobo culture in completing this last minute replacement task.

My grandson Quinn and his father Blake had booked their Mt Kenya climb for March 27, 2021. On March 26th, Kenya's President, responding to a rapid escalation of Covid cases in the country, announced a travel ban between our Nakuru County and Laikipia County where Mt Kenya is located. That task is still being postponed, until travel opens up. But, as with all tasks we give our children, we have to be flexible when we run up against unforeseen obstacles.

Richard's son, Jordan (Jack's oldest grandson), also came of age during Covid 19 and his big adventure task of mountain climbing had to be delayed. At the same time, during Covid, he experienced a once-in-a-lifetime chance to see God work in the adoption of his Rwandan sister – a task Richard and Ericka had been working on for ten years. Jordan got to see that God's timing and faithfulness is not necessarily confined to a year. The year he was given challenged him to develop new skills in technology and sparked an interest in a potential career, which he may never have explored. Trusting God with the timing and setting and circumstances of the 12 Tasks is something both parents and sons and daughters have to adjust to.

Examples from Lives of Those Who Have Done 12 Tasks

Melissa Eager recalls the night when their daughter Rachel had to camp out alone as one of her tasks: With minimal instruction, she scurried around the kitchen and pantry preparing her evening meal for her solo camp out, a very simple tin foil dinner to be slow cooked over the fire. Her dad had instructed her in setting up the tent earlier in the day and the fire pit was set. Her camp site was only a few meters from our house.

As the sun sank swiftly in the equatorial African sky, we left her alone to build her fire and spend the night in the outdoors by herself, assuring her that the door was unlocked and that we were close by. She was excited and ready to go! As the flames of her fire flicked and died down, she placed her meal on the glowing embers. A stray dog, roused by the scent of potential food, skulked in the nearby shadows, shaking her confidence. In boldness, the canine trotted out, drawing nearer...too close for comfort in the increasing darkness. Deciding she would rather eat half raw veggies than keep company with a hungry, underfed dog, she scampered into the tent and zipped up.

After eating what should have been a delicious meal but turned out to be less than yummy, she climbed into her cozy sleeping bag. In the confines of the tent, strange shadows weaved about the thin fabric walls as the trees creaked in the moonlight. Alert to every sound, sleep eluded her. Eventually, the eerie whoop of hyenas began to sound through the night. Though not close by, that was it. Out of her sleeping bag, out of the tent and a sprint to the house found her safe and warm in her own bed for the rest of the night.

While our daughter's first attempt at this task may have failed, it gave us an opportunity to talk with her and encourage her. Her two older brothers were a part of this as well. As she had already succeeded at setting up the tent, preparing a meal and building a fire, the next night, she retired to the tent at bed time and while it wasn't an easy night for her, she made it through the night in the tent. Task completed successfully. So if, at first, something doesn't work, don't give up on it. Try it again or adapt the task. Or even change it altogether. You want your child to succeed and to be able to celebrate it.

***

I (Shel) went to a mission conference in Nairobi in January 2020 and at tea time, I saw a young girl named Elizabeth selling what she called 'cub cakes' – tasty and cleverly decorated cupcakes designed to look like young lions or cheetahs. I recognized Elizabeth's mother Brandy Johnson nearby and I knew Brandy was doing 12 Tasks with her daughter. So I asked if this was one of her daughter's tasks. Brandy said it was. The task involved creating the business, baking the cupcakes and selling them. I went to Elizabeth and encouraged her in completing her tasks by buying a whole tray!

***

When I met Mutugi M'Narobi recently, I asked if he had planned 12 Tasks for his daughter, after he had written to me for advice on how to do this. He said they had started on her first task – running 30 miles. Mutugi noted that his daughter was not too excited about running, and getting the task done required him to run with her to encourage her. But they were doing it – together!

***

Our children will not like every task and they may balk or complain. Melissa Eager had this experience with her daughter Rachel. "She would roll her eyes. 'Why do I have to do this? I don't want to do this.' But having gone through 12 Tasks with our two sons, we understood the value. We also felt that this would be something that if she didn't complete, she might regret it later on. We worked together on the list of tasks and made some adaptations along the way. It didn't go quite as smoothly as it had with our sons, but in the end we succeeded. I say 'we' because this takes a lot of time and commitment on the part of parents. As a parent, it's important to realize that you might mess up along the way too, or wish that things had happened differently. But that can all contribute to the process of teaching our children what it means to become a young man or a young woman."

Some tasks are unique for your time and space and some are once in a lifetime opportunities which can't be missed. Jordan

(Jack's oldest grandson, Richard's son) had such an opportunity when it came to the adoption of his Rwandan sister.

Richard and Ericka co-founded an educational organization in Rwanda called Wellspring and enjoyed life with their three boys until Richard was invited to become the vice-president (Student Life) at Trinity Western University. The Taylors had been trying to adopt for ten years and then Covid hit – making this venture seem impossible. Door after door had been shutting over the years as agency after agency shut down and options all but dried up. In the middle of the impossible, the possible became a reality.

The family had purchased six Agaseke baskets several years before even though there were two parents and three sons – making five. The sixth basket stayed nestled inside. At a moment of doubt Jordan drew his family's awareness to the reality of their dream exemplified in that sixth basket. It kept hope alive.

So, Jordan was given the task of documenting the incredible journey of his new sister's adoption and all the answers to prayer that came with it. Rwandan friends, a lawyer, an airline pilot and many more jigsaw pieces fit together in the effort and resolve to expand this family. Jordan combined the story with 58 pictures to create and present a graphic journey that is a precious keepsake for this family. He was able to use his interest in computers, photography and language to showcase strengths that came from a once in a lifetime experience. Sharing this treasure with his grandparents allowed them to vicariously share in the miracle.

The story Jordan documented only increases in significance when one realizes that days after the final hurdle was finished, country borders and international flights all shut down because of Covid. The family squeaked back into Canada intact as a family.

We encourage all our participants to pay attention to those unique experiences that will provide a foundation for building skills and living memorials that will last beyond the limits of the one year of tasks. The tasks are not meant to be overwhelming but to be significant for the child and parent sharing these together.

Perhaps a health crisis, a natural disaster, a trip, or participation in an experience has provided you with a chance to sharpen a skill or ability that could be highlighted. Consider how life is offering up surprises which you can embrace and grow through. Creating a lasting memoir of a family experience allows the task to provide a lasting memory for everyone to enjoy over and over again.

Of course, you can also plan for every task so there are no surprises if that is your bent. All we are saying is to be open to that unexpected moment which will give you the flexibility to share something unique to you. These are the 12 tasks for your child and they are the tasks to help both parent and child see themselves in ways you may have missed if you hadn't been intentional.

This family of six continues to celebrate the goodness of God and the grace of people he put along the way. They have had many exciting opportunities to affirm their family ties. None of them had any significant symptoms during that time. Miraculous is the only word left to say.

In addition to writing his book about the adoption, one of Jordan's 12 Tasks was riding 200 km with his father Richard over three days in the Okanagan region of British Columbia. This really tested Jordan's perseverance. The first day they started out from Penticton, BC on the hottest day of the year. Richard had underestimated how difficult the hills would be for Jordan and how scary the traffic would be along the side of the road. At one point, Jordan ended up falling off his bike and skinning up his knee and his elbows. But he pushed through and two days later father and son celebrated together on Shuswap Lake outside of Salmon Arm, British Columbia. The memories made together as father and son during that time were priceless.

Jordan is highly creative and loves technology. Richard and his wife Ericka wanted to use 12 Tasks as a way to encourage this talent while steering Jordan towards using technology to create social good rather than merely consume content. So one of Jordan's tasks was to make a promotional video highlighting a challenge in the world and a potential solution. Jordan decided to enter a contest held by a non-profit organization to create a new promotional video for their medical mission and received a third-place prize for his efforts.

Jordan also memorized the book of Philippians. At first, he was very motivated and quickly memorized the first two chapters. But once he reached Chapter 3, it got tougher, and he started to lose interest. Richard's encouragement and setting up clear markers for memorizing a certain number of verses each day helped to get to the finish line. Though it took great effort, Jordan found the task to be meaningful for his spiritual growth as a teenager.

Jordan also interviewed four men from four different

generations on the topic: how to be a godly man. He then took time to write down his reflections and identify key things he wanted to emulate from each of the men he interviewed. This helped improve his communication skills, approach adults with greater confidence, and learn from the wisdom of men in his life who had walked the journey ahead of him.

CELEBRATING THE 12 TASKS

11

Creating a Memorable Celebration

When your son or daughter finish their 12 Tasks, they deserve to be celebrated. The moment should be shared with close family, friends, and the 12 Tasks Community. John and Melissa Eager realized how important it was to be sure the grandparents could be involved in the celebration. Melissa wrote: "Celebrating the completion of the tasks with significant people is important as well. Living overseas made celebrating with grandparents challenging but while things worked out fairly easily for this to happen with our first two kids, Covid really got in the way of this with our third. We celebrated our daughter's 13th birthday on the actual birth date, but we delayed the ceremonial aspect to completing her tasks by several months, as we felt it was important for the grandparents to attend. It may not have meant as much to our daughter at the time, but it meant a lot to the grandparents."

Work with your child to select a location, put together an invitation list, and identify a program. You may already have some important traditions from your family background you would like to incorporate. Feel free to do so but try to ensure you include the following important elements of a 12 Tasks Celebration:

Reward, Remember, Exhort and Commission.

Reward: Choose a special gift for your son or daughter that will always remind them of their accomplishment and what it means to be an adult. For Richard this was a special purity ring, to remind him part of his journey meant saving his sexuality for marriage. For Shel's family, having already given a purity ring as part of the 'talk,' we gave our kids a Swiss Army knife. We felt it was an appropriate symbol to show we felt they were responsible enough to handle and care for a special (and potentially dangerous) tool. Think about what would be special for your son or daughter and present this gift as part of the 12 Tasks Celebration.

Remember: The same 12 Tasks book that became a memorial for receiving the challenge should also become a memorial for completing the 12 Tasks. Prior to the celebration you might want to finish putting in photos or mementos into that book. My (Shel's) son Blake's completed 12 Tasks book has a sample of his Velcro mosquito net repair kit that he had designed as one of his tasks. He had created it to complete his Task of creating a potential business opportunity to solve a problem. He had created handy Velcro squares that you could use to cover gaping holes in mosquito nets while traveling in East Africa.

You might also want to create a separate photo book or video documentary together of the 12 Tasks journey. During the Celebration, take some time to reflect, tell stories, and recount the joys and challenges of the 12 Tasks Journey. Encourage your son or daughter to share his or her own experiences and thank those present for their support along the way.

One of the values of the keepsake books recording the 12 Tasks was seen in our (Jack and Gayle) recent family get together in 2021. We were celebrating the fourth of our grandchildren to hit 13 in the same year. Out came the 12 Tasks book from my daughter Michelle to see her tasks. And with the book came the stories – the good ones and the others. The favorite one continues to be the hardest. For Michelle, Mt Kenya was the most horrific of memories. She claims still that if she thinks about it, she'd have to book a counseling appointment. The thing that matters is the Certificate of Achievement framed and signed by Warden Bongo Woodley for April 5th through 8th, 1997.

Michelle and Laura climbed the mountain with Jack, with a few friends from Canada, and with another two other missionary families initiating their daughters. The rain was so bad that the mountain truck could not get to the first hut. It continued to slide into the ditch repeatedly and regardless of how many tree branches and rocks the rangers tried to put under the tires the big beast was going nowhere. We were up too far to head back so we had to grab our gear and hike to the first cabin, walking uphill through mud as slick as ice. We had several falls along the way. We were soaked, muddy and exhausted by the time we reached the starting point for the hike.

One of Michelle's pictures has her in hiking boots, bundled in a red toque, an extra-large borrowed white jacket on top of everything else, standing next to a giant Lobelia while her younger sister Laura stands cross-armed in a lighter jacket leaning against her tall friend, smirking as if this task will be nothing. In the background stand the daunting white tops of the three peaks. Laura did conquer that task with little trouble while Michelle struggled the whole way up and back. I had to walk with hiking poles and two sets of braces on my knees.

The weather was miserable most of the way up and two people ahead of us were carried down dead before we made it half way up. One was the university-aged porter carrying our gear. Another was a tourist. We took the altitude sickness seriously, but we kept going. I think Michelle might have been as sick as I was on my first attempt but I didn't want her living with regrets so the guide and I nudged her up the snowy scree on that final morning as she dry heaved to the top. I pushed her over the final snow hill to pose on top. The camera was as frozen as the rest of us so the memento had to be captured by others.

On the way down, Michelle frequently sat and didn't want to move. We fell behind the group but had to get all the way down in that one day with the rain pouring and the rivers of water streaming all around us. Rock hopping across small rivers added to the energy output. When we finally got within a kilometer or so of the truck, we noticed lion tracks had crossed the road behind those in front of us. It added a little adrenaline rush to finish what we had started. Back at the lodge, we posed on top of the sculpted model of the mountain holding up our certificates. We had accomplished a memory.

One of the things I (Jack) did at the beginning of each book was to sketch a cartoon drawing of my child featuring the different tasks they had to do. Now Richard has asked that I do the same for his oldest son Jordan to start his book. These are unique ways to add memorable twists to each book and mark it as special.

Tasks for Michelle included climbing Mt Kenya; reading through the Bible in a year; doing 50 hours of free babysitting; writing 24 different full page letters to different friends and relatives; memorizing Matthew 5 and 6 from the Sermon on the Mount; making a complete dinner for company including the ordering, buying, cooking and cleaning up; learning to change a bed every two weeks and keeping her room neat without being asked; purchasing material and making a pair of shorts; reading 12 novels of her choice and 3 of our choice; making a pizza dinner for her sister's birthday and writing out her plans ahead of time; visiting 5 elderly people for an hour each while taking them a creative gift; writing a paper explaining the character, talents, abilities, interests and desires that God gave when He made Michelle while listing the possible careers in which these could be used and developed.

Capturing the 12 Tasks can build memories for a lifetime and serve to stimulate the next generation of 12 Taskers. Take advantage of your creative side with video or photo collages, powerpoints and photojournals.

My (Jack's) eleven-year-old granddaughter, Natalie, heard me talking to her mother (Michelle) about the book and asked to see it. She thoughtfully focused on each picture and the tasks her mother had gone through. The challenges were clear but seemed to be focused on what had happened in another country far away in a time long gone.

Even though she, her younger sister and her older brother have not done 12 Tasks, they have been in karate for several years, working their way through the various belt levels. They have already gone through a significant number of swim levels. They are being trained each day in biblical disciplines, are active in church and are limited in their exposure to social media and the larger community. Parents will find different ways to initiate their children into adulthood. Some will spread the challenge over years and through various disciplines. The important thing is that there is intentionality and relationship building in the effort.

However, when Natalie saw her mother's 12 Tasks book, it brought back memories and conversation about how the 12 Tasks is more than just a series of activities during a tough year of her mom's life. It had been a formative time in her life, which encouraged her to raise her children and to involve a cultural mind-set that carries into the next generations where new and unique challenges are being faced.

Exhort: Words of affirmation mean so much to a young man or woman. At the celebration event, it is valuable to select a few adults (and perhaps a peer) who are willing to speak into his or her life and encourage them. You can also open up a time for guests to speak and share what they appreciate most about your child.

Gary Smalley and John Trent, in their book, *The Blessing*, state: "the terrible fact is that most people who have missed out on their parents' blessing have great emotional difficulty leaving home. It may have been years since they have seen their parents, but unmet needs for personal acceptance can keep a person emotionally chained to his or her parents' home, unable to genuinely cleave to another person in a lasting relationship. For this reason many couples never get off the ground in terms of marital intimacy."[23]

---

23   Gary Smalley & John Trent, The Blessing (Nelson: Nashville, TN. 1986) p. 19.

There are five elements listed in *The Blessing* which would fit in well with the 12 Tasks time of celebration upon the completion of your son or daughter's tasks. These are Meaningful Touch; A Spoken Message (or messages from several of those involved); Attaching High Value to the One Being Blessed; Picturing a Special Future for the One Being Blessed; An Active Commitment to Fulfill the Blessing.

Meaningful touch conveys warmth, acceptance, affirmation and well wishes. A spoken message is meant to breathe life into the soul of the successful Task finisher. To have numerous voices affirming specifics about his or her life will alert them that others see, notice and welcome the strengths they exhibit in a time when world changers are needed. The confidence that arises cannot be measured. Placing a high value on your child is a way to honor them, to treasure them, to remind them of their worth. Word pictures are important vehicles to communicate memorable images of value to the one being recognized. Drawing out a preferred future in an image that your young man or young woman can hold onto is not mere visualization, which could discourage them if the goals you set are too lofty. This picture conveys your familiarity with them, their interests, their hopes, dream and desires and it motivates them toward the pursuit of excellence. The last step conveys the responsibility that comes with blessing and the completion of the task. Growing up is not completed because of 12 Tasks.

Commission: Speak words of blessings over your child. Make it clear that moving forward you recognize them as a young adult and will treat them accordingly. Make it clear that this will include more freedom to make decisions but also more responsibility. This time will also ideally include a time of prayer and asking God for his guidance and direction in your child's life as they move forward.

Without the blessing, Smalley and Trent[24] say that children may become seekers of intimacy who are seldom able to tolerate

---

24   Smalley & Trent, The Blessing, pp. 143-146.

it. They may become shattered, troubled over the sense of loss and acceptance, prone to fear, anxiety, depression and emotional withdrawal. They may become smotherers, sucking the energy out of their close relationships and yet still emotionally empty. They may become angry, emotionally chained to birth parents, never forgiving or forgetting what they've missed out on. They may become detached, protecting themselves from letting anyone get too close, embracing loneliness instead. They may become driven, embracing life as perfectionists, workaholics, picky and demanding over the smallest details, always reaching for an elusive accomplishment to fill the void. Then there are those who become seduced, looking for love in all the wrong places, trying to meet a legitimate need in an illegitimate way.

This is a lot of emphasis to say that this final tribute and gathering and affirmation of all the meaningful voices makes a lot of difference. Make use of video clips, emails or whatever means you have available to get key individuals in the room and recorded for remembrance. Words spoken now can make a huge difference later.

A commissioning should include significant prayers by significant persons laying their hands on the young man or woman as appropriate. Again, Smalley and Trent have wisdom to share: "Wise parents will model this practice in bestowing the blessing on their children. When they say, 'May the Lord bless you,' they are first recognizing and acknowledging that any strength they have to bestow the blessing comes from an all-powerful God...We are all prone to be inconsistent, and we stumble occasionally in providing the elements of the blessing for our children. In contrast, God remains changeless in His ability to give us strength to love our spouse and children in the way we should."[25]

Conclusion

Some of our kids were a bit embarrassed by the hoop-la at the completion ceremony for the 12 Tasks. But they still

---

25   Ibid, p. 101.

remember the event. It is important to mark the finish line well. Make sure there's a reward. Make it a special memory. Encourage and exhort your child for the years ahead and commission them into adulthood (or at least into their turbulent teens) with a blessing. And then continue to pray and work with your child as they move on up the path to adulthood. It won't be easy, but it will be worth it.

Recently we shared our experience with 12 Tasks at our international fellowship in Naivasha. As part of the service, I interviewed three of our grandkids and our son Reid, the first person we know to have completed 12 Tasks himself and then to have helped all of his children complete their 12 Tasks. Reid's youngest, Max, had completed his tasks earlier in the year and we'd had his completion celebration with a barbecue for family and friends and cliff diving into the Malewa River. Reid acknowledged that doing the 12 Tasks with his four children had been a challenge and very time-consuming for him and his wife Sandy. However, his last piece of advice that he shared at our fellowship was this: "If you have a chance to do something like this with your kids, do it! It's worth it!"

WRITING THE STORY OF YOUR 12 TASKS

We've come to Chapter 12 in our book on how to do the 12 Tasks. You'll find it's mostly blank. That's because it's up to you to write your own story as you embark on your own 12 Task adventure with your child. We've given you stories on how 12 Tasks began and the importance of doing 12 Tasks. We've given you clear steps on how to create your own 12 Tasks as a rite of passage for your child. We've also given you examples from the lives of others who have used 12 Tasks to help their children on their quest towards adulthood. Now it's up to you write the rest of your story as you help your child take this important step towards becoming an adult. Enjoy the journey!

To help those who are doing 12 Tasks, we have created a website – 12tasks.org On this website you will find resources to help you on your journey.

We'll also be posting the experiences of others who have done 12 Tasks, or are in the midst of doing 12 Tasks. Visit 12tasks.org to read more about 12 Tasks and to share your own stories.

In addition, you can order our two novels that center around 12 Tasks from Amazon.com.

12 Tasks of Manhood by Jack Taylor

Test of the Tribal Challenge by Shel Arensen

APPENDICES

Appendix A

The How-To Manual for 12 Tasks

12 Tasks are designed to take place over a one-year period when your son or daughter is about to enter their early teens. You will need to start working with your son or daughter to design 12 Tasks about six months in advance of this period.

This how-to manual is divided into three sections and is intended to give you the practical steps necessary to do 12 Tasks successfully with your son or daughter.

DESIGN IT walks you through the process for putting together your customized 12 Tasks with your son or daughter. It will include tips on approaching your child, finding a mentor, building a 12 Tasks community, assessing your son or daughter, and prioritizing the tasks.

DO IT helps you chart out the timing for completing 12 Tasks, provides some tips on how you can sustain momentum, and how you can encourage your child appropriately in the process without controlling him or her.

CELEBRATE IT helps you put together a Celebration Ceremony for your child so their family, peers, and community can affirm them in their success.

	DESIGN IT	**DO IT**	**CELEBRATE IT**
Steps	- Commit to doing it with your son or daughter. - Find a Mentor - Recruit others to join your journey. - Assess your child. - Plan 12 Tasks together.	- Begin 12 Tasks. - Check-in regularly. - Do some Tasks together in community.	- Design and hold a Celebration Ceremony for your child.
Tools	- Outline for a Mentor. - 12 Tasks Community. Understanding Your child. - Picking Tasks.	- 12 Tasks Book.	
Timeframe	**4 months**	**12 months**	**1 Day**

Appendix B

What to Expect in your Child's Teen Years

The first years of adolescence are some of the most challenging transitional times in human experience as the move from childhood to adulthood happens physically and to some extent psychologically. A parent's encouragement toward independent decision-making is a crucial help along the way. The next generation's world changers are envisioning what else could be. Peer relationships can be scrambled under new emotions and hormones. A healthy youth group with experienced leaders can provide a positive culture in which relationships can be explored safely.

Communication channels should be nurtured and guarded between parents and emerging adolescents. A young teen is transitioning from parental pressure to peer pressure during a time when boys may be traumatized by erections, wet dreams and clumsiness while girls deal with menses, irregular periods and developing breasts. Teens who display direct healthy person-to-person communication often do so because of solid family communication patterns. They also tend to be efficient in their task orientation, have clarity around parental roles and be closer in relationships. It may help to invite adolescents into establishing the details of family contracts around the area of chores, rules, privileges and consequences for violations. Frequent renegotiation, with love, grace and acceptance, at significant milestones is advisable to maintain a sense of ownership as the youth matures.

The health of the parental relationship is vital for the well-being of the emerging teen. 12 Tasks will not magically fix deep rooted issues entrenched from unhealthy family dynamics. Some parents who seek to have their own needs met through the child may fear that this stage of life means abandonment and may prevent healthy independence through smothering, spoiling or overprotection when it comes to decision making.

Parents who model a healthy love between themselves will give their offspring a chance to experience a healthy spiritual, emotional and physical love in their own relationships. Healthy spiritual, emotional and physical traditions will also yield positive long-term benefits which may already be seen during the 12 Tasks. Children tend to adopt and adapt the value system established in their own homes. An unhealthy system will yield anxiety, fear, insecurity, depression, guilt and other factors which will undermine the attempt to mentor and coach your child through the Tasks.

If a child has grown up in a home with rigid expectations, overly demanding standards, and harsh rules coupled with constant blame, accusation, judgment and condemnation a warped understanding of reality is likely. A healthy dose of encouragement, praise, thanks, appreciation and even the asking for forgiveness will provide the nurture, stability and supportive structure needed for the turbulent years ahead.

Josh McDowell and Dick Day, in their book, *How To Be A Hero to Your Kids*, speak of the telltale signs of perfectionism. They note that perfectionists have an all-or-nothing mentality, wanting to do their task perfectly and delaying things if they don't think they can accomplish it well enough. Sometimes they don't try for fear of failure. A parent should be aware of how this can impact the completion of the tasks. Perfectionists can get down on themselves and feel that this is unacceptable. Taking risks may be a point of resistance if your child has this tendency.

"There is a real difference between allowing children freedom to fail and demanding that they strive for perfection, which only puts them in a double bind. On one hand, they learn to play it safe and not take any risks. They don't come up with anything very original. On the other hand, they strive for perfection in certain regimented and organized ways.

"Everyone is going through a process called life. We are walking through that process, but we will never arrive, because life is a journey, not a destination. As we walk along, most of us are set on accomplishing something. We have goals. We are results-oriented... It's good to have goals and it's good to want results, but if goals and results are reached at the expense of enjoying the process, then you have missed life. We all need to be enthusiastic about the process of life, and learn to pass our enthusiasm - not our extreme expectations - along to our children."[26]

Positive Parenting features acceptance, appreciation, availability, affection, accountability and authority. The 12 Tasks will not be a pleasant experience for you or your child if your parenting style is autocratic, permissive or indifferent. Ephesians 6:4 encourages parents not to exasperate or overcorrect their children so they find obedience difficult. Rules need to be made out of relationship, for a specific purpose, and with clear direction and reason. Don't set up a system where your child must misbehave to get attention. There should be natural consequence or logical consequences if things go awry.[27] It would be unfortunate to see the success of 12 Tasks undermined by unnecessary relational conflict.

Some of the conflict may be eased if parents take time to understand the challenges happening within the brain of the adolescent. Gregory Keck, in his book, *Parenting Adopted Adolescents*, says:

"The adolescent brain is very much a work in progress — just like the adolescent himself — and is responsible for fueling and dousing the fires that are so typical at this age. One part of the adolescent brain, the limbic system, is responsible for impulsivity, risk-taking, sexual drive, and emotional responses. Another part of the brain, the prefrontal cortex, is responsible for emotional and behavioral regulation, task accomplishment, organization, planning, rational thinking, and decision making. Imagine that these two components are engaged in an ongoing tug of war throughout adolescence.

"Brain research is exploding, and it is revealing that the

26   Josh McDowell & Dick Day, How To Be A Hero To Your Kids, (Word: Dallas, TX, 1991) pp.99-100
27   Ibid, pp. 196-199.

prefrontal cortex - the reasoning regulating device - is not fully developed until after age twenty. As a result, it's easy to see what is happening in the adolescent brain. The seat of emotion, the limbic system, is fully fired up, and the prefrontal cortex that's supposed to mitigate what the limbic system produces is still asleep at the wheel, not fully capable of doing its job. No wonder adolescents sometimes appear not to have any good sense at all, and no wonder they calm down dramatically in their twenties. That's just the way the brain is wired to work."[28]

"So, if parents expect good, solid judgment and decision making from their adolescent, they may be disappointed. However, if they know that the adolescent's brain is not working at full capacity to regulate his behavior, they will realize they need to step in and serve as the adolescent's training wheels until he is able to function properly by himself."[29]

28   Gregory C. Keck, Parenting Adopted Adolescents (NavPress: Colorado Springs, CO, 2009), pp. 21-22.
29   Ibid. p. 22.

Appendix C

Stages of Emotional Growth
A strong family where husband and wife model appropriate physical attention and affection for each other will help boys navigate and mitigate identity challenges. A father must know, himself, that we as human beings are not merely biological beings who must live out all our urges, desires and fantasies. Because we 'feel' something doesn't mean we must 'do' something. Modeling the spiritual fruit of self-control before your son will encourage him to deal with his own challenges.

Tracking Stages of Emotional Growth – (based on the work of Peter Scazzero – *Emotionally Healthy Spirituality*)
Growing into emotional maturity is a crucial step for adults if they are to expect this from their offspring. The chart below is one way to track your emotional maturity and that of the one you hope to disciple. An honest evaluation of yourself in this area can be humbling.

What does the following tell you about your own emotional maturity? Help your child identify where they might be on the chart.

Emotional Adolescents
- Tend to be defensive
- Are threatened and alarmed by criticism
- Keep score of what they give so they can ask for something later in return
- Deal with conflict poorly, often blaming, appeasing, going to a third party, pouting, or ignoring the issue entirely
- Become preoccupied with themselves
- Have great difficulty truly listening to another person's pain, disappointments, or needs
- Are critical and judgmental

Emotional Adults
- Are able to ask for what they need, want, or prefer – clearly, directly, honestly
- Recognize, manage, and take responsibility for their own thoughts and feelings
- Can, when under stress, state their own beliefs and values without becoming adversarial. Respect others without having to change them
- Give people room to make mistakes and not be perfect
- Appreciate people for who they are – the good, bad, and ugly – not for what they give back
- Accurately assess their own limits, strengths, and weaknesses and are able to freely discuss them with others
- Are deeply in tune with their own emotional world and able to enter into the feelings, needs, and concerns of others without losing themselves
- Have the capacity to resolve conflict maturely and negotiate solutions that consider the perspectives of others.

A father must be consistent in his own appropriate affection and attention to his son. To increase a son's level of anxiety or fear by over-reacting with personal rejection or restriction will not accomplish the protection or correction you wish to give. A son needs to see that his father is strong enough to handle him as he moves toward the edges of independence through the exploring of the world he is entering.

Teaching strong core values and demonstrating them in family life from the earliest years is important. If this hasn't been the heritage of the home then it is important to gently and graciously move in this direction before launching your son into his 12 tasks. A boy needs a strong foundation from which to step out.

Qualities are not absolutes for male or female but are general strengths reflecting the whole character of God who encompasses all traits from strength to gentleness. Fathers need to understand that God has designed their sons (or daughters) for specific tasks and roles in the world and their natural bent and character need to be accepted and nurtured toward godly expressions.

A father's investment begins in the early years of his son's life and the 12 Tasks are part of the journey of a healthy bonding that can one day turn into a lifelong friendship.

Appendix D

What if My Child Is Adopted?

Adopted children may eventually question their sense of identity, belonging and value. "Why did my natural parents give me up?" may be a question that writhes in their souls – spoken or unspoken. Behavioral testing to try out the resiliency and staying power of the adopted parents may stretch the bonds of love but a commitment toward the five elements of blessing listed earlier can help make the difference in the sense of belonging, security and self-confidence.

Gregory Keck, in *Parenting Adopted Adolescents*, says: "An adolescent who was adopted will probably have additional components in this separation and individuation process. Unless the child was adopted at birth, he probably has had some level of trauma-either minor or profound-which impacts the quality of the relationships he develops. If his original foundation was laid in a chaotic family, relationships will be somewhat fragmented. If he has a developmental foundation that was created by both a birth family and an adoptive family, the separation process will be more complicated. He may, in fact, be able to separate more effectively from the adoptive family than from his birth family. He may retain the birth family's component because it keeps him connected to their familiarity, and he may even use it as part of his individuation process. If that occurs, the adoptive parents may feel as if they are being replaced by the adolescent's family of origin. In the case of an adolescent identifying with a dysfunctional or criminal birth family, the adoptive parents would have legitimate concerns regarding their child's choices."[30]

"Some adolescents engage in the individuation process like

---

30   Gregory C. Keck, Parenting Adopted Adolescents, (NavPress: Colorado Springs, 2009), p. 23.

a whisper, while others go through it with a shout. Figuring out the difference is simple: Growing extra-long hair is a whisper; dying it bright green and adding multiple facial piercings is a shout." [31]

Richard, Jack's son, adopted a daughter from Rwanda. Transracial and transcultural adoptions add interesting consideration for parents facing the 12 Tasks. While one's race is biologically determined, "culture is a system of values, beliefs, attitudes, traditions, and standards of behavior that govern the organization of both individual and group behavior. Culture is adaptive; it is created by groups of individuals and incorporated into group life to assure survival and well-being to the group's members." [32]

Keck identifies seven core issues experienced by all adopted persons. "These fundamental issues are loss, rejection, guilt/shame, grief, identity, intimacy/relationships, and control/gains. Regardless of circumstances of an adoption - infant, older child, international - children are affected by loss, which is the cornerstone of every adoption. Losses related to adoption are lifelong, life-altering, and intergenerational. These losses and how they are handled set the parameters within which an adopted child's life is played out. The losses intermingle with day-to-day attitudes, biases, and perspectives as they unfold alongside the child's development. Adopted children vary in their response to these losses based on temperament, personality style, gender, subsequent experiences, and other factors, such as medical conditions and intellectual functioning." [33]

When it comes to the 12 Tasks, each family's culture will form a framework for which tasks will be focused on. The adolescent will also be aware of their peer culture, their school culture, their faith culture, and perhaps their ethnic culture as well.

"An adolescent in a transracial adoption will almost definitely explore racial differences in a way marked by the zeal

31   Keck, p. 23
32   Keck, p. 115.
33   Kech, p. 49

and intensity typical of his age. If his parents have addressed race as an integral component of life throughout his childhood, his exploration may be more tempered. If, on the other hand, the family operated as if race didn't matter, the adolescent will most assuredly make it matter, and he will probably do so as loudly as possible."[34]

It appears like wisdom to incorporate some element of understanding with regard to racial heritage somewhere among the tasks. More than ever, race has risen to the surface as a key identity marker and parents should not ignore this reality if they truly want to help their child transition into a healthy adulthood. At the same time, each child will have their own level of curiosity and their own timing to deal with issues of identity. It might be good to propose an identity project for your child among the initial choices but to let them choose. One option might be: "How does adoption affect a young person's view of their own identity? Talk to six people adopted across cultures and write a paper of your findings. Include your own sense of how your adoption has impacted who you are."

---

34   Kech, p. 117.

Appendix E

How I Have Helped My Boys to Become Christian Men

Vern S. Poythress, Ph.D., Th.D. 1999

God gave me two boys to raise, Ransom and Justin. Ransom is now 14 years old and is already a Christian man. Justin is a Christian boy 12 years old, and is training to become a man before he is 13.

What is going on here?

Something special. I believe that God has given to my wife Diane and me a special idea about raising boys, an idea that may be of use to you if you have sons in your family. We have created a special celebration and ceremony to introduce them to Christian manhood. This celebration we call "Bar Jeshua," that is, "son of Jesus." This celebration marks the point at which a boy becomes a man, a mature disciple of Jesus.

Is such a thing weird? We don't think so. Let me tell you about it.

The Idea and the Challenge

Almost every culture in the world has something to mark the difference between a boy and a man. A boy goes through a "rite of passage," after which he becomes officially a man. The rite of passage may involve an ordeal, a test, or a training period of some kind. The boy who has reached a certain age must kill a crocodile, or train with a bow and arrow, or go on a long journey alone, or join in a dangerous hunt with the men.

When does a boy become a man in white American culture? When he gets a driver's license? When he graduates from high school? When he moves away from his parents? When he can vote? When he gets his first full-time job? When he is 21? When he gets married? When he owns his own home?

No one can say. There is no clear point of transition. There is no one "rite of passage." One of the unfortunate effects can be that boys are insecure. They don't know when they are men. Again and again they may try to prove that they are "grown up." Sometimes they may choose destructive ways - join a gang, go hotrodding, learn to smoke, get drunk, take a girl to bed.

What do we do to give proper guidance? I know and you know that there is no magic formula. God must be at work in teaching us and our boys, and he must be the one who causes them to grow (1 Cor. 3:7). But you and I can plant and water.

I decided that one way I could help my sons was by showing them what it was to be a man. What is a man? What marks maturity? In the Bible, true maturity does not consist in being able to kill a crocodile! The true maturity is spiritual. It is wisdom in knowing God and his will, and being able to carry it out in your life (Prov. 1:1-7).

I must set an example by my manhood. I must be like Paul, who said, "Follow my example as I follow the example of Christ" (1 Cor. 11:1). That is an awesome challenge. I fail to live up to the biblical standard. But part of being a man is being able to admit it when I fail and then to ask forgiveness.

Passing to Manhood

In addition to all the regular things that must go into Christian living, I decided that my boys should have a rite of passage. It involves training and testing. It is not easy for them. They must prove themselves to be Christian men.

My son Ransom, 13 years old, has been through it. He knows that he is a man. He knows it not only because he worked and sweated at it, but because we had a celebration at the end. We sent out invitations. At the party, in the presence of about 90 people, his friends and our family friends, we reviewed some of the testing, and then I declared in front of everyone that he was now a man. "As your father, I declare that you are no longer Master Ransom Poythress. You are Mr. Ransom Poythress. You are now a man."

The change of name is significant. White American culture

still has a tiny fragment in which it recognizes manhood. According to formal etiquette, a boy is "Master" until he is 12; after that, he is "Mr." (Mister). One of my Latino friends tells me that they have a celebration of manhood at the 12th birthday. The Jews have a "Bar Mitzvah" for a boy when he is 13.

The Jews became a model from which we attempted to learn. Though Diane and I are not Jews by birth, Jesus is a Jew. The Jews of the Old Testament are therefore our spiritual ancestors. In addition, we live in a neighborhood with many Jews. So in our neighborhood the idea of having a ceremony for manhood was not strange. We created a celebration called "Bar Jeshua," "son of Jesus," by analogy with "Bar Mitzvah," son of the commandment, the Jewish celebration for entering manhood. We can also point to the incident recorded in Luke 2:41-50. At 12 years old Jesus, our Savior and Representative, shows his manly maturity in his understanding of the Bible and his understanding of his role.

The Bible does not require us to imitate slavishly any one culture. But we see wisdom here.

So what did we do? We tried to do the normal things that go into Christian parenting. But in addition, we told the boys from an early age about the Bar Jeshua we were planning for each of them. We told them that they would become men when they were 12. They were going to have to train for it beforehand.

The Training

In what does the training consist? Christian manhood is the goal. The training must match the goal. So we set for them projects. They acquire and demonstrate skill in each of several overlapping areas.
1. Knowledge of the contents of the Bible.
   - Know the names of books of the Bible in order.
   - Know Bible history.
   - Read the Bible all the way through.

- Know main themes of biblical books.
- Understand how biblical teaching centers on Christ.
- Know Greek and Hebrew (amount of knowledge tailored to the child's ability)

2. Memorization of selected verses and passages of the Bible.
3. Knowledge of the major teachings of the Bible (doctrine).
   - Memorize a children's catechism as a summary of doctrine.
   - Be able to explain doctrines and respond to questions using one's own words.
4. Personal piety.
   - Using devotional materials
   - Prayer diary
   - Day-long personal retreat for prayer and fasting with Daddy
   - Growth in understanding of means for overcoming sin
5. Projects of service and mercy.
   - Serving the church; serving the needy.
6. Wisdom in dealing with various spheres of life.
   - Finances: tithing, drawing up a year-long budget; checkbook balancing; investing.
   - Etiquette: table etiquette, greeting etiquette, letter etiquette, conversational etiquette, sexual etiquette.
   - Apologetics: answering questions and objections about Christian faith; understanding the Christian world view and the main competing worldviews and ideas in the United States.
   - Sexuality: knowing Christian teaching and standards for thoughts and actions. Understanding how God designed male and female bodies.

They work on these areas over a period of years. Many times we just integrate the work into our family devotional times. At other points we have periods where they have concentrated study in one area. When the boy is 11 years old, we assess progress. If our boy is honestly far from ready, we are willing in principle to put things off for another year. But if he is showing more maturity, we have a time of more concentrated preparation.

In the two or three months before the Bar Jeshua celebration, we enlist our pastors, young people's leaders, and (in my case) my seminary professor friends to test the boy privately in each of the areas (1)-(4). I am present at these tests to provide moral support, but not to coach my boy on the answers. We also reserve the fellowship hall at our church as a site for the coming celebration. We send out invitations. We draw up a program sheet and buy decorations and food.

The Celebration

The day of the Bar Jeshua celebration is a Saturday, so that more people can come. I explain the celebration to all present.. Our boy reads a short passage from the Hebrew Bible and explains it (as does the Jewish boy at Bar Mitzvah). The boy reads a short passage from the Greek Bible and explains it. The people who previously tested our boy come and give a "mini-test" as part of the celebration. But our boy already knows that he has passed the private tests, so he does not have to fear the result. We sing our boy's favorite hymn. We pray for him. I declare that he is a man. Then we eat and converse. That's it. Many of the guests bring gifts for the boy, because they can see that it is like a big birthday celebration.

Thinking It Through

What do our boys think of it? They are intimidated. At times they get discouraged. "It's too hard," they say. "I don't like it." "Why do I have to do this?" We did make it hard. Manhood is not easy. This life is not easy for a Christian. We keep encouraging them. But we also challenge them. And we avoid showing any sign of giving in to the pressures around us. "Why are we different?" they say. "This is what Mommy and I have decided to do. God has given us a responsibility to train you to be a man. Because you are in this family, this is what you have to do."

We have to strike a careful balance. We have to match the projects to our children's capabilities. We can't make the work so hard or so time-consuming that it exasperates our children or is just an oppressive burden (Eph. 6:4). On the other hand, we don't want to give way to the lazy feeling of much of American culture, where many people just float along, without clear goals, and seek to be entertained and avoid hard work. Other people in America work very hard, but for unworthy goals: to be "successful," to get fame or wealth. We encourage hard work toward the worthy goal of serving Christ. We try to hit the positive note of encouragement many times for every one time that we have to criticize them. But we don't hide the fact that we are swimming against the cultural tide.

Having Another Man in the House

What happens after our boy becomes a man? He has the privileges of a man. The privileges must be real and meaningful. This part is scary for Diane and me. But we told ourselves, "It is better to give our young man lots of freedom now, while he is still at home. At 14 he is still young enough to come and ask us for advice. He is young enough to know that he doesn't know everything. For him to explore under these conditions, when he is still in our home, is far better than waiting until he goes away to college and we don't see him or talk with him about all the challenges."

When our boy becomes a man, lots of changes take place in many areas, some big, some small. As a man, he no longer needs a baby-sitter. He can baby-sit younger children himself. He sets his own bedtime and rising time. He decides when he does his homework and how long he works on it. He decides what TV programs he watches and how long he watches. He can (at first with supervision) teach a children's Sunday school class. He participates in the "family council" when my wife and I discuss, plan, and make important decisions. He can buy and care for his own pet. He excuses himself from the table rather than being asked to be excused. He buys his own clothing, school supplies, and gifts. He pays rent once a month, based on an estimate of his share in the utilities, food, and other costs. And he has an allowance to match these new responsibilities! In addition, if I pay him to do an extra job, I pay him at a going rate - at least the minimum wage, and more than that for jobs that are demanding.

But even when our son is a man, he is still part of the family and still lives with us. We love him just as much. We kiss and hug him just as much. We play together. We have certain rules that we would have for anyone living with us, even people outside the family. We expect him to be at meals on time. We expect him to be considerate of other members of the family. If he goes somewhere, we expect to know where he is. On Saturday night we meet as a family and assess the week. We continue to talk with him about where he is spiritually. If we see sin in his life, we will exhort him as we would exhort an adult who was on intimate terms with us. We continue to encourage one another and teach one another as fellow believers in Christ (Col. 3:16; 1 Thess. 5:14).

Christianity, after all, does not isolate adults from one another, but puts them in the body of Christ (1 Cor. 12). In that body we are answerable to one another. So Ransom's freedom is not freedom for immorality. If I were to see my brother in Christ filling his mind with raw TV programs, or neglecting his homework, or even just staying up too late every night and then dragging in the morning, we would sit down and talk. We would ask, "Is this really wise for a Christian man?"

I must say that, so far, we are pleased. It has been work for us. But Ransom is a man now. Sure, he has energy and interests like many other fourteen-year-olds. But in matters that count, he acts like a man. Not perfectly. Not without some stumbles and signs of immaturity. But he does. We noticed a big change right after his Bar Jeshua.

Some Resources That We (Vern and Diane) Used

- Larry Burkett, *Surviving the Money Jungle: A Junior High Study in Handling Money* (Gainesville, GA: Christian Financial Concepts, 1995).
- *Catechism for Young Children: An Introduction to the Shorter Catechism* (Philadelphia: Great Commission, n.d.)
- Paul Little, *Know What You Believe* (Colorado Springs, CO: Chariot Victor, 1987).
- Paul Little, *Witnessing; How to Give Away Your Faith* (Downers Grove, IL: InterVarsity, 1996).
- Susan S. Macaulay, *How to Be Your Own Selfish Pig* (Colorado Springs, CO: Chariot Victor, 1982).
- Theodore C. Papaloizos, *Alfabetario: Pre-School Reader* (n.l.: Papaloizos Publications, 1990). (Introduction to Greek letters and pronunciation.)
- Amye Rosenberg, *Alef Bet Mystery* (New York: Behrman House, 1980). (Introduction to Hebrew letters and pronunciation.)
- R. C. Sproul, *Choosing My Religion*, tape series (Orlando, FL: Ligonier Ministries).
- R. C. Sproul, *Objections Answered*, tape series (Orlando, FL: Ligonier Ministries).

Appendix F

The Talk on Purity

By the time your child is ten they have likely had many encounters or exposures to sexuality in some form. Hopefully, you've had some opportunity as a parent to communicate the basics of reproduction, sexuality and male-female differences. If you haven't taken the opportunity, then likely someone else has and your own values may already be undermined.

It's never easy for a parent to give 'the talk' to their child. I (Shel) know that my parents never brought up the subject of sex with me. However, I did notice a new book in the bookshelf by my mother's reading chair one day, when I was about 15. It had a catchy title. *How Far Can I Go*. No one was home, so I flipped through the book. It was a Christian book about sex and how to set limits while dating and remain pure until marriage. I got hot and sweaty and quickly put the book back into the bookshelf, scared that someone might come in and see me looking at it. I wondered why my mother wanted to read such a book. But the book kept drawing me back. Eventually, a few days later, I slipped it out of the bookshelf and hid it in my room and read it. After I finished it, I snuck it back into the bookshelf. I realize now my mother had placed the book deliberately for me. I'm sure she was secretly pleased when she saw I had purloined the book! So that was the extent of what I received from my parents about purity.

When we decided to do 12 Tasks with our boys, I knew I needed to do better with my boys. We felt it was an appropriate time in their lives to include some savvy, biblical advice on sex. In our case, we tagged the talk to the Obelix all-you-can-eat meal at the Carnivore. I still remember watching each of my boys as their eyebrows went up, amazed that their Dad was talking about sex, man-to-man, right there in the restaurant!

After the talk, I gave each of our boys a Zanzibar slave ring and told them to wear it as a symbol that they were to be bond slaves to the Lord and follow his instructions to avoid all kinds of sexual impurity and to wait until marriage to enjoy sex.

In the 1980s and 1990s there were several books on dating and abstinence which created what became known as the 'purity culture' in the evangelical Christian world. Christian parents encouraged sexual abstinence in their children by passing on a purity ring. Some contemporary Christian leaders trash and mock the practice as a feeble effort by parents trying to guilt their child into abstinence. But that wasn't our purpose. We wanted our children to understand the biblical mandate to avoid sexual immorality and I did my best to honestly express the joy of sex in a married relationship and the hurt that could result if the gift of sex was misused. I felt the ring was a powerful symbol. The Zanzibar slave rings, which are made in a zig zag with sharp points, can be uncomfortable, so our boys didn't wear them regularly because of sports and some got lost. But I do believe the talk did give each of our children a strong foundation on how to love and care for someone of the opposite sex. It was embarrassing for them, I'm sure. It was uncomfortable for us as parents. However, it gave us a chance to share openly about sex with our children and to leave the door open for future discussions as they continued to mature.

I just met a friend who is a college biology professor. He knew we had done 12 Tasks and he wanted to do something similar with his son, but he just didn't have time to do it. However, he knew the importance of giving his young teenage son a man-to-man talk on sex. So he planned a one-day climb up a mountain in the Adirondacks in New York. When they had conquered the mountain, a big physical challenge, my friend then shared with his son about the 'birds and the bees' (he's a biology professor after all) as they trekked down the mountain. He admits it was mostly a one-way conversation, but he was able to explain things clearly to his son – and leave the communication pathway open for future talks as needed.

There are plenty of books or online resources you can check out if you're not sure how to explain about sex to your child. As a parent, you won't give the talk perfectly. It will be uncomfortable. Your child will be embarrassed and probably want you to stop. Don't be discouraged. Prepare yourself. Choose a quiet place. Tie in your talk with a Task – maybe a celebratory meal like we did, or while on a challenging hike as my friend did. The most important thing is to open the conversation about sex and purity with your teen.

Bibliography – Resources for Your Journey

Arterburn, Stephen and Stoeker, Fred with Yorkey, Mike, Every Young Man's Battle: Strategies for Victory in the Real World of Sexual Temptation, Waterbrook: Colorado Springs, Colorado, 2003

Blackaby, Henry and Richard, Spiritual Leadership. B&H Publishing: Nashville, Tennessee

Borthwick, Paul, But You Don't Understand: How to Know You're Doing the Right Thing With Your Kids, Nelson: Nashville, Tenessee, 1986

Bruner, Matthew, "When Does a Boy Become a Man?" Strugglingteens.com, May 2, 2007.

Chapman, Gary, Choose Greatness: 11 Wise Decisions That Brave Young Men Make, Northfield: Chicago, Ilinois, 2019

Chapman, Gary, The Five Love Languages of Teenagers: The Secret To Loving Teens Effectively, Northfield: Chicago, Ilinois, 2016

Clark, Jeramy and Jerusha, Your Teenager Is Not Crazy: Understanding Your Teen's Brain Can Make You a Better Parent, Baker: Grand Rapids, Michigan, 2016

Dobson, James, Bringing Up Boys: Practical Advice and Encouragement for Those Shaping the Next Generation of Men, Tyndale: Wheaton, Illinois, 2001

Drescher, John, Seven Things Children Need: Significance, Security, Acceptance, Love, Praise, Discipline and God, Harold: Scottdale, Pennsylvania, 1976

Elkind, David, All Grown Up and No Place to Go: Teenagers In Crisis, Addison-Wesley: Menlo Park, California, 1984

Elkind, David, The Hurried Child: Growing Up Too Fast Too Soon, Addison-Wesley: Menlo Park, California, 1981

Elmore, Tim and McPeak, Andrew, Generation Z Unfiltered: Facing Nine Hidden Challenges of the Most Anxious Population, Poet Gardener: Atlanta, GA, 2019

Fitzpatrick, Joel and Thompson, Jessica, Mom, Dad…What's Sex?: Giving your kids a Gospel-Centered view of Sex and our Culture, Harvest House: Eugene, Oregon 2018

George, Jim, The Man Who Makes a Difference: 10 Keys to a Life of Impact, Harvest House: Eugene Oregon, 2010

Keck, Gregory C., Parenting Adopted Adolescents, NavPress: Colorado Springs, Colorado, 2009

Kesler, Jay, Ten Mistakes Parents Make with Teenagers: And How to Avoid Them, Wolgemuth & Hyatt: Brentwood, Tennessee, 1988

Laurent, Robert, Keeping Your Teen in Touch With God: Why Teens Turn Away from the Church and How You Can Prevent It, David C. Cook: Elgin, Illinois, 1988

Lehman, Kevin, The Birth Order Book: Why You Are the Way You Are, Revell: Old Tappan, New Jersey, 1983

Lehman, Kevin, quoted in Dear Abby, Independent Press Telegram, January 12, 1981

McCartney, Bill, What Makes A Man? NavPress: Colorado Springs, Colorado, 1992

McDowell, Josh and Day, Dick, How To Be A Hero To Your Kids, Word: Dallas, Texas, 1991

McDowell, Josh and Dottie, Straight Talk with your Kids about Sex, Harvest House: Eugene, Oregon, 2012

McKee, Jonathan, If I had Parenting to Do Over: 7 Vital Changes I'd Make, Barbour: Ulrichsville, Ohio, 2017

McKee, Jonathan, More than just The Talk: Becoming your kids' go-to person about sex,
Bethany House: Bloomington, Minnesota, 2015

Marshner, Connie, Decent Exposure: How to Teach Your Children About Sex, Legacy Communications: Franklin, Tennessee, 1994

Mercola, Joseph and Lerner, Ben, Generation XL: Raising Healthy, Intelligent Kids in a High-Tech, Junk-Food World, Nelson: Nashville, Tennessee, 2007

Murrow, David, Why Men Hate Going to Church, Nelson: Nashville, Tennessee, 2011

Priebe, Barton. Adopted by God: Discover the Life-Transforming Joy of a Neglected Truth (KDP 2021)

Rohr, Richard, From Wild Man to Wise Man: Reflections on Male Spirituality, Franciscan Media: Cincinnati, Ohio, 2005

Sanders, Bill, Tough Turf: A Teen Survival Manual, Revell: Old Tappan, New Jersey, 1986

Schimmels, Cliff, Oh No! Maybe My Child Is Normal! Shaw: Wheaton, Illinois, 1991

Schimmels, Cliff, What Parents Try to Forget About Adolescence, David C. Cook: Elgin, Illinois, 1989

Simon, Mary Manz, How to Parent Your Tweenager: Understanding the In-Between Years of Your 8 to 12 Year Old, Nelson: Nashville, Tennessee, 1995

Sloat, Donald E., The Dangers of Growing Up in a Christian Home, Nelson: Nashville, Tennessee, 1986

Smalley, Gary and Greg, The DNA of Parent-Teen Relationships: Discover the Key to Your Teen's Heart, Focus on the Family: Colorado Springs, Colorado, 2005

Smalley, Gary and Trent, John, The Blessing, Nelson: Nashville, Tennessee, 1986

Stoeker, Fred, with Yorkey, Mike, Tactics: Securing the Victory in Every Young Man's Battle, Waterbrook: Colorado Springs, Colorado, 2006

Townsend, John, Boundaries With Teens: When to Say Yes, How to Say No, Zondervan: Grand Rapids, Michigan, 2007

Waliszewski, Bob, How to Raise Media Savvy Kids With Love, Not War, Focus on the Family, Colorado Springs, Colorado, 2011

Yoder, Wes, Bond of Brothers: Connecting with Other Men Beyond Work, Weather and Sports, Zondervan: Grand Rapids, Michigan, 2013

If you found this book helpful please consider leaving a review on Amazon and consider purchasing some of the other books by these authors. Please also recommend it to others in your social media world. Thank you. If you have questions for the authors or would like to participate in a Facebook forum please email jackataylor@live.ca

Made in the USA
Monee, IL
27 July 2025